Selling Online

How to Start a Home-Based Business Selling Used Books, DVD's and More Online

Patrick Leo

P & L Publications
www.pandlpublications.com
Brea, California

ISBN-13: 978-0-578-03031-9
ISNB-10: 0-578-03031-4
Library of Congress Control Number: 2009907007
Printed in the United States of America.

Limit of Liability, Warning, and Disclaimer

TABLE OF CONTENTS

Introduction 1

Chapter 1: Finding Items 5

Your Junk 5

Garage and Yard Sales 6

Estate Sales 8

Used Bookstores 9

Thrift Stores 10

Police Auctions 11

Post Office Auctions 14

U.S. Treasury Auctions 14

BookSaleFinder.com 15

Library Sales 16

eBay.com 16

Classifieds 19

Storage Rental Auctions 20

Craigslist 20

New Items? 21

Chapter 2: What to Buy and How Much to Pay 23

Books 23

Fiction 30

Non-Fiction 31

Rare and Collectible Books 31

A Final Word on What Books to Avoid 32

CD's, DVD's, and Video Games 32

    CD's 33

    DVD's 34

    Video Games 34

Other Items 36

Pre-Order Reports 37

Scanners 37

Chapter 3: Listing Your Items 39

Bulk Sales 40

Individual Sales 43

    Amazon.com – www.amazon.com 43

    Half.com – www.half.com 60

    Alibris – www.alibris.com 63

    Abebooks.com – www.abebooks.com 66

    eBay - www.ebay.com 68

Chapter 4: Shipping Your Orders 83

Postage 83

    Online Postage Companies 87

Shipping Supplies 91

A Few More Shipping Tips 96

Chapter 5: Customer Service 99

Shipping 99

Item Description 100

Returns 101

Refunds 105

Asking for Feedback 106

Removing Negative Feedback 107

Chapter 6: Inventory Management 109

The SKU System 109

Cleaning Out Your Closet.. 110

Is Storage an Issue? 112

Price Adjusting... 113

Chapter 7: Automation 115

Automation Software 117

Scanners 121

Chapter 8: Setting Up Your Business 123

Types of Businesses 124

Sole Proprietorship.. 125

Partnership 125

Limited Liability Company 125

Corporation 126

Business License and Sales Tax................................... 126

DBA... 126

Sales Tax Permit 127

Further Business and Tax Resources 127

Basic Accounting.. 128

Appendix 1: Seller Website List 131

Appendix 2: Buying Items for Resale Website List 133

Used Items... 133

Remainder Book Wholesalers 133

New Products 134

Appendix 3: Online Postage and Shipping Suppliers 135

Online Postage Companies... 135

Shipping Supply Companies 135

Shipping Scales 137

Scanners 138

Appendix 4: Examples of My Sales 139

Books 139

CD's, DVD's, Video Games 143

CD's.. 143

DVD's 145

Video Games 146

Appendix 5: Generic Listing Templates 149

Books 149

CD's.. 150

DVD's 151

Video Games 151

Appendix 6: Profit Analysis 153

Appendix 7: Amazon Best Practices 157

Listing Items and Inventory Management 157

Order Management.. 158

Fulfillment 159

Customer Service.. 159

Security 160

Appendix 8: Recommended Reading **161**

References **163**

Index..**165**

INTRODUCTION

Selling online has never been easier or more profitable. I started selling used books, CD's, DVD's, and video games online in 2003. I found the business of selling used items online so profitable that I started my own home-based business and have been selling online from the comfort of my home ever since.

This book is going to show you how to start a home-based business selling used items online. The best part about the strategies I am going to show you is that you do not even have to own or maintain a website. Companies, such as Amazon.com, allow third party sellers to resell anything in their catalogue as well as add new products to their website.

If you have never sold an item online before then you are coming to the market at the perfect time. There have never been more websites where sellers can list their products or more places where sellers can go to find products to sell online. I am going to show you the best websites where you can list your products; I will also walk you through how to use each of those websites to make the most of each sale. In addition, I am going to show you the best places to find plenty of items that you can resell online.

I am going to give you every tip I have learned and show you the secrets to my success. Even though I specialize in selling used books, CD's, DVD's, and video games, I also sell other items such as electronics and a variety of household items. After reading this book, you will know what items are the easiest to sell and how to make the most from each sale.

Types of Sellers

There are different categories of people that sell online. This book is structured to help any type of seller maximize their potential in the online marketplace.

Casual Seller

A casual seller is someone who could be trying to clean out the junk in their garage or perhaps is looking to clean out some space in their bookcase. Do you have a lot of books, CD's, DVD's, and video games that you do not think will ever be read, watched, or played again? Is your garage used as storage for junk instead of what it was built for, your car?

If so, you may be a casual seller. This book is going to show you how to clean out that junk and make some cash while you are at it. I will show you websites where it is free to list your items; many sites do not charge a commission until you actually sell something.

I will also walk you through the best ways to ship your stuff, what types of supplies you are going to need, and the best places to get them. You will find tips to easily deal with the Post Office and other shipping services as well as what to expect when you sell and ship your items.

The online marketplace, I believe, was actually created with the casual seller in mind. After reading this book, you will find that selling online is easy, simple, and profitable.

Part-time Business Seller

Perhaps you are a casual seller who wants to take it to the next level. Well, it has never been easier to start your own business. You will learn how to set up your business with little cost to you. I will walk you through how to get a business license, a resale license, and some basic tax information you will need to be aware of.

The biggest difference between the casual seller and the part-time business seller is that the part-time business seller needs to be on the hunt for new items to sell. You will soon find you can sell your own used stuff so fast that you will be low on inventory; so, I will show you the best ways to find more items to sell. There are a variety of websites, as well as local events, where items are constantly being auctioned off at little value.

A part-time home-based business is a great idea for someone looking for supplemental income. The best part about selling used items online is that you can dictate how busy you want to be. If you only want to put in a few hours a week then you will only need to find and list a few items each week. On the other hand, if you want to put in 10 – 20 hours a week you can simply list more items online.

Full-time Business Seller

Full-time business sellers are the professionals out there. You will find them selling on just about every available seller outlet. As a casual or part-time seller you will be competing against these pro's but do not worry, there is plenty of business out there for everyone.

If, after rising through the ranks of casual selling to starting a part-time business, you feel it is time to sell online full-time, this book will guide you along that process. For example, is it better to keep your business a sole proprietorship or incorporate? How can you find and lock in enough inventory to continue to sell at high levels?

The strategies discussed in this book will enable you to keep up with the other professionals out there. You will learn how to automate your listing, inventory management, shipping, and customer service functions so you can concentrate on finding new inventory and still find time to relax every once and awhile.

This book is going to help you no matter what type of seller you are. I have no doubt that, using the tips in this book, your first online sale is going to be but one of many. There is no reason to hold off any longer: read this book, get online, and make some money!

CHAPTER 1:
FINDING ITEMS

Your first step to selling online is going to be finding items to sell. This chapter will give you the knowledge you need to find different auctions in your local neighborhood as well as what websites you can go to in order to find items to sell online.

Your Junk

The easiest way to find items to sell is to take a look at all the stuff that you are just hanging onto; it could be books that you will never read again or movies you want to get rid of. You can also take a look in your garage to see what you are storing. Do you have any electronics, TV's, or furniture? All of these items can find another home as well as put some dough in your pocket.

Books, CD's, DVD's, Video Games

Books, CD's, DVD's, and video games are going to be your instant income machines. These items are the easiest to find, list online, and ship to your customers. I make most of my money selling in those categories and I encourage you to focus your selling efforts in those categories as well.

Your first step in organizing your junk is to gather all your books, CD's, DVD's, and video games. Oh, and by the way, VHS tapes still sell too. So, if you have any of those you want to get rid of then put them in a sell section. My advice is to clear a spot in your garage and designate that as your sell section, or if you have an empty room you can put all the items you want to sell in there for now.

Make sure the items you are selling are in decent condition. A big part of your success in selling online is making your customers happy. Happy customers leave good feedback and good feedback leads to more people wanting to buy from you. So, if you have any CD's, DVD's, or video games that are completely scratched then it is best to just trash them. Once you have everything organized that you want to sell then you are ready to get your shipping supplies and list your items, both of which I will be discussing in the following chapters.

Garage and Yard Sales

Garage and yard sales are great places to find additional items to sell. If you are not happy just selling your own junk online then why not sell someone else's?

Finding garage sales is a local specific activity. You will want to look through classified ads and even drive around your neighborhood looking for garage sale signs.

Depending on where you live, there may even be free classified newspapers such as the PennySaver. I do most of my business in Southern California and find that many people advertise their garage sales in the PennySaver. The PennySaver is distributed in a few different states and you can check them out at www.pennysaverusa.com.

The PennySaver is known as a classified advertising publication. If you do not have the PennySaver where you live you will most certainly have something similar. Check out where the newspaper vending stations are and you will often see one station which has free classified advertising publications.

Garage Sales Tips

- **Get there early!** Most of the good stuff is going to sell fast. If you know of a few garage sales you are going to hit that day then try to prioritize which ones you want to go to first. Sometimes the classified ads will describe some of the items that will be sold. You can use that to prioritize. If your goal is books then look for the ads that list books. I have found that most people fail to list in their ads that they have books for sale. Used books, for some reason, seem to have little to no value to the owners which makes them great buys.
- **Do not be afraid to haggle.** The beauty of a garage sale is that the owner wants to get rid of his/her junk. At the end of the day, they do not want to be left with anything. In fact, most people either trash or send their leftover garage sale items to a donation center. I will go into what to pay for items in the following chapter but it is always best to pay as little as possible. The less you pay, the higher your profit margin.
- **Come on back.** Sometimes it pays to come back to a garage sale at the end of the sale. This is the point where the owners are going to be the most desperate to unload their junk. For the most part, they will be almost giving it away. The only problem with waiting until the

end of the sale is that most of the good stuff is usually gone.

- **Introduce yourself.** Have some business cards made and pass them around to the owners of the garage sale. Let them know that you are always in the market for used books or whatever other type of product you want to specialize in.

Estate Sales

You can find some real bargains and some great items to sell at estate sales. A true estate sale is exactly as the name implies; someone or some company is trying to sell an entire estate or house full of items. The items are usually sold individually or in lots. An estate sale occurs when someone may have passed away and no one knows what to do with all their stuff. Perhaps the relatives cannot take all the stuff and have hired a company to perform an estate sale or are performing the estate sale themselves.

At a typical estate sale you will walk through the house and everything in it will be for sale. These estate sales are advertised, for the most part, in your local newspaper's classified section. Estate sales are more competitive than garage sales as there are a lot of deals to be made.

Estate Sales Tips

- **Get there early!** Just as with garage sales, the most valuable items are going to be gone in the first few hours.

- **Haggle.** It is still a good idea to try to lower the sales price of items you are thinking of buying.
- **Return to the sale the next day.** Most estate sales are two day events. I have found that on the second day the operators usually lower their prices significantly. The incentive is also there for the operators to unload everything that is left over.
- **Introduce yourself.** Usually estate sales are performed by companies on behalf of the family of the estate. You can leave your business card with the operators and ask them to give you a call about future estate sales. In fact, most of the companies that perform the estate sales let you sign up to be notified by e-mail of up and coming sales.

Used Bookstores

If you know of any used bookstores around your neighborhood you can use them to find used books to sell online. Most used bookstores get swamped with books but have a limited space in which to store all those books. Because of this, they may be willing to sell you some of their overstocked inventory at a deep discount.

It never hurts to speak to the owner or manager and try to get them to sell you some of their inventory. You can leave them with your business card and let them know that you are always in the market for volume sales. Most owners will always listen to a buyer who is willing to buy in volume since shelf space is a large problem for traditional brick and mortar used bookstores.

If not, you can always scour the used bookstores for mispriced items. Sometimes the bookstores will list all paperbacks at $0.75, $2.00, or some other fixed price. You might be able to find books listed at that fixed price that you can later sell for $5.00 online. I will get into how to price your purchases in more detail, but if you have a cell phone with internet capability you can look up individual titles on the Amazon.com Marketplace, or another website, to see what they are selling for used. I will also explain what titles you should be looking up in the next chapter so you do not have to waste your time flipping through every book in the store.

Thrift Stores

Thrift stores are the shops that sell donated items. The two most famous that I know of are Salvation Army and Goodwill. Both Salvation Army and Goodwill have retail stores where you can buy a variety of items. I think the best things to buy from them are books, CD's, DVD's, and video games.

Similarly to used bookstores, thrift shops typically price their items at a flat rate. For example, all DVD's might be $5.00 and all paperback books might be $1.75. Using a device as simple as your cell phone, if it is internet enabled, will allow you to look through their inventory and find items that you can resell online.

The thrift shop retail stores might also let you buy in bulk at a discount. These stores are routinely swamped with used books, in particular, and are looking to unload their stock. Both companies also have central donation and distribution centers. The stores can request inventory from the main centers or, if they are overstocked, they can send some of their inventory to the central centers. The central donation centers often will have weekly, bi-weekly, or monthly auctions.

These auctions are where you can find some of the best deals available. The location and availability of the auctions is subject to change so you will need to visit the websites of both Salvation Army and Goodwill to find the exact locations, dates, and times.

I will say that it pays to make as many friends as you can with the workers at the donation centers. They will be able to tell you the best times to get to the auctions and what new items might be on the auction floor. So, use the business card tactic whenever possible; at the retail stores try to speak to the manager and let him/her know you are a professional who is always in the market for bulk sales, and at the auction center you can leave your card with the auctioneers and ask to be notified of upcoming auctions.

The website for Salvation Army is:
www.salvationarmy.com.
The website for Goodwill is:
www.goodwill.org.

Police Auctions

One of my favorite ways to get items to resell is through police auctions. Just think about all the things people have had confiscated or stolen that have never been claimed; after a certain amount of time the authorities have to have some way to get rid of all that junk piling up. Some departments have their own auctions while some use different companies to handle the auction for them.

The one thing I love about police auctions is that there is often new stuff mixed in with old stuff. Of course, there are also times when the stuff is complete junk but that is the risk taken when buying bulk items at an auction. You usually do not know exactly what is in an auction except for the type of item and the quantity.

You can find police auctions in a number of ways. One way is to go to your local police department's website. This can usually be found by going to your city website and then clicking on the police department link. For example, I took a look at San Diego's city website, which is a city in California close to where I live: www.sandiego.gov. I noticed they had a link to their police department and even a link to their police department's auctions: www.sandiego.gov/police/auctions.shtml.

The San Diego Police Department's website has information regarding the schedule of the auctions and even a preview of what items to expect at the auctions. Other police departments will have similar information. You may even have to call the information line for the department and ask if they have auctions or how they handle their auction process. In addition, do not forget to look into your local sheriff departments as well and use the business card tactic whenever possible.

You can also find out about police auctions by reading your local newspaper. The notifications about the auctions are usually in the classified section.

Another way to get access to police auctions is through a police auction website. The one that I think is the best and that I know has affiliations with a number of police departments is PropertyRoom.com. Their website is www.property-room.com. I highly recommend you check out their website and use their service.

PropertyRoom.com is an online auction service that serves over 1,500 law enforcement and public agencies nationwide. On their website you can find just about anything from bikes to collectible coins to electronics. They put the goods that I love (books, CD's, DVD's, and video games) in the following categories:

Books are found under Everything Else > Media > Books & Magazines.

CD's are found under Everything Else > Media > Movies > CD's.

DVD's are found under Everything Else > Media > Movies > DVD.

Video games are found under Everything Else > Media > Video Games.

As with other auctions, most sales are "as-is". The company does a good job of explaining the possible defects to the items so you can better determine a value for the goods. If you buy CD's, DVD's, and video games there will probably be times when you get items that are too scratched up to sell; however, for the most part, the items will be in a condition that allows you to resell them online.

Another alternative to finding police auctions is through paid services. If you search police auction on the internet you will most likely come across these services. For a monthly or yearly subscription they will send you information regarding auctions nationwide.

I do not use these services as I find all the auctions I need by doing a little extra work described in this section. You can always find these auctions by contacting the police department itself or scanning the classified section of the newspaper every day. If you still want to check out a subscription service then one that I have seen recommended is DEAauctions.com at www.deaauctions.com.

Post Office Auctions

You might be able to find great deals on books, CD's, DVD's, and video games at post office auctions. The Post Office gathers all unclaimed, undeliverable, and damaged merchandise and auctions them off. Currently, the Post Office only holds large auctions at the Atlanta Mail Recovery Center.

The Post Office has an auction in Atlanta about once a month. You can go to the USPS auction website to find the exact address, dates, and times. The USPS auction website is located at:
www.usps.com/auctions.

U.S. Treasury Auctions

The United States Treasury also holds auctions in which it sells seized or other U.S. Government property. The items available through these auctions include everything from collectibles to electronics. You will need to go to the upcoming auction website in order to find out what items are coming up for sale and what location the next auction is going to be at.

You can find this information by going to the U.S. Treasury website at:

www.ustreas.gov/auctions/treasury/gp.

The United States Department of the Treasury also has an online auction format similar to eBay where you can bid on items. That website is:

www.govsales.gov.

BookSaleFinder.com

Book Sale Finder is a great site to go to in order to find any number of large book sales in different parts of the U.S. No matter where you live, you can probably find a book sale somewhere. This site lists book fairs, library sales, and other book auctions.

There are also links to a number of book seller services including listing software and scanners. If you are a full-time seller it will make sense for you to invest in a wireless scanner of some type. This will enable you to scan the barcode of any book you come across and instantly find the price. Again, if you have a cell phone with internet access you can look up any book, but it is more time consuming than just scanning the book. I will dive more into the topics of scanners and listing software later.

The website for Book Sale Finder is:

www.booksalefinder.com.

Library Sales

If you go to Book Sale Finder you will find a number of library sales. You will also find library sales by routinely checking classified ads in the newspapers and by contacting your local libraries. You can find some great deals at library sales and, just as with the garage and estate sales, it pays to get there early. You will also want to be selective in the books you buy and I will walk you through that in the next chapter.

The one issue that I have with a library sale is that, well, you are going to find ex-library books. Most, if not all, ex-library books are going to have a couple things wrong: a stamp on the inside cover or first page stating which library the book belonged to and tape around the spine of the book. The tape around the spine is actually beneficial as it keeps the spine in excellent condition for a used book. However, you will need to disclose that the item you are selling is an ex-library book when you list them on websites such as Amazon.com. In addition, to be in full compliance with listing regulations on Amazon.com, the highest you can grade an ex-library book is "good" condition. Despite having to disclose that it is an ex-library book, I still recommend going to library sales as a way to increase your inventory because most of the books will still sell online.

eBay.com

I will be discussing how to use eBay to sell your items shortly but did you know you can use eBay to buy items to sell? This works great for books, CD's, DVD's, and video games. However, there is a lot of junk floating around as bulk sales too. The key term here would be "caveat emptor"; in other words, buyer beware.

For those that are unaware of what eBay is, I want to explain a few things and discuss how to use eBay to buy items to resell. eBay is an auction website. The website is full of other companies and individuals. There are some regulations as far as what you are allowed to sell but, basically, anyone who has something to sell can list their item for sale on eBay.

People generally buy items on eBay just as they would in a standard auction; by bidding on the items. A typical sale will last seven days and the highest bidder will be the winner of that auction. He or she then pays the seller.

It is free to register on eBay. This will allow you to buy and sell items. If you do a lot of transactions on eBay you will also want to have a PayPal account. PayPal is owned by eBay and is a transaction service company. I pulled this from their "about us" section on their website, "PayPal is the faster, safer way to pay and get paid online. The service allows members to send money without sharing financial information, with the flexibility to pay using their account balances, bank accounts, credit cards or promotional financing."(1)

PayPal makes it easy to buy and sell on eBay and other sites that accept PayPal. You do not need a PayPal account to buy on eBay though. You can always pay with a credit card.
The web address for eBay is www.ebay.com.
The web address for PayPal is www.paypal.com.

Since we are using eBay to buy bulk lots for resale we can go to the main website: www.ebay.com. On the top left you will see a categories section. Click on the drop down and you will see a large list to choose from. You can click on the "books" link and that will bring you to a "categories within books" section. On the bottom right of that section you will see a "Wholesale & Bulk Lots" link.

When you click on the "Wholesale & Bulk Lots" link you will see all the auctions available for books in bulk lots. On the left-side of that page you can refine your search even further by clicking on "books" and then you can choose the amount of books you are looking for. You can perform the same process for CD's, DVD's, video games, or just take a look at everything under the "Wholesale & Bulk Lot" category.

eBay is definitely worth taking a look at. Having said that, you need to have some way to estimate what the values of the books are. Some sellers are just selling hundreds of worthless books so they do not list what titles are available. If you do not know what you are buying then it makes it hard to estimate what to pay. My advice is to stick with sellers that list their books in their auction detail page so you can look some of the titles up to see what they are worth. The same advice goes for CD's and DVD's. When you are just starting out you do not want to be stuck with 150 DVD's that are on the bottom of every site's sales list.

One of the things I like about eBay is that it is a very interactive site. Buyers will leave feedback about sellers and vice versa. This gives you an opportunity to check out the seller's history and credibility before you buy. If you see a seller with a low feedback score you will probably do yourself some good to find another seller. You will find a seller's feedback score when you click on an auction. You can then click on the seller's ID to see their history on eBay.

If you already have an eBay account then you are all set to start searching for deals. If not, I recommend signing up. I will be going into how to use eBay to sell in a later chapter. I also think having an eBay account is necessary if you are going to be selling items other than used books, CD's, DVD's, and video games. And best of all, it is free to register!

Classifieds

The classifieds section in your local newspapers is a great place to find out about upcoming auctions, garage sales, and estates sales. You should also use the classified publications, like PennySaver, discussed earlier.

In addition to finding out about upcoming events, you can advertise to buy. Some professional sellers will advertise their services to buy used items in the classified section. This is a good idea if you are set up as a business and if you have your own website. You can direct people to your website where you should have them fill out a request form where they describe their items. This gives you a great idea of the potential value before you proceed.

This works best for used books, CD's, DVD's, and video games. The people that respond to your ad should be encouraged to give you the titles of the items for sale. If not, when you contact the seller you should have some sort of scanning equipment, which I will discuss later, so that you can quickly value the items.

This strategy is mainly for the professional sellers. If you do advertise to buy in the classifieds take the necessary precautions to protect yourself. If you are going to someone's house to value their items then bring someone along with you, or at least let someone know where you are going to be.

Storage Rental Auctions

Do you know those self-storage facilities? I think the biggest chain of self-storage facilities is Public Storage: www.publicstorage.com. Sometimes something will happen to the person who is renting out a storage unit; perhaps they have passed away, were arrested, or they just cannot pay the fee but have no room for their stuff. Either way, the self-storage facility will often auction off those contents.

Usually the storage facility will put in a notice in the local newspaper. The notice can be found in the classified section with the heading of "notices". If you do not see any you can always do an internet search for local self-storage facilities and give them a call regarding their own auction procedures. Better yet, if the facilities are nearby you can show up with your business card and introduce yourself as a buyer of used goods. They might be able to give you a call when upcoming auctions are going to be taking place.

Craigslist

Craigslist is an online classified website. It is also free to sign up and create posts. You can use this similar to the newspaper classifieds. You will be able to find items in your area and can advertise your services on the website. The website address for Craigslist is: www.craigslist.org.

New Items?

The focus of this book is in selling used items online, but I think it is worth mentioning that you can sell new items on all of the websites I will be discussing. In the Appendix section of this book I have listed a few places where you can purchase new items to sell online.

To purchase from these sites you will need to be set up as a business and be registered with your state tax board as a reseller. For the most part, selling new books, CD's, DVD's, and video games online is a low profit margin business. It is difficult to make money selling on the websites I will be discussing due to the number of sellers trying to do the same thing. The cost of purchasing the items is going to be a lot higher than if you just focused on used items.

One technique that booksellers use to sell new books online is to buy remainder books. Remainders are books that a bookstore does not want to carry on its shelves anymore but cannot return them. Remainders can be bought at a wholesale discount from some of the sources listed in the Appendix.

The problem with remainders is that most will not be in hot demand; after all, they are getting fired from the bookstore shelf. The other issue I have with remainders is that it takes a fair amount of research to find out what remainders are available for sale, how much you can buy them for, how many sellers are trying to sell the same book, and what price do you think you can sell it for. In addition, most remainders will have a remainder mark which is usually a mark made with a black marker to the bottom of the book; the mark is not a huge deal but you are going to want to disclose this to your buyers when you list the book for sale. Furthermore, to be in full compliance with Amazon.com listing procedures, the highest grade a remainder book can receive is "like new" even if it is technically a new book. Amazon.com states that since the book is not in pristine condition it cannot receive a condition grade of "new".

You can also buy remainder CD's to sell online. Remainder CD's are going to have a different mark to them; most remainder CD's are going to have a small cut out in the corner of the jewel case. The cut out does not damage the CD but it will require you to disclose the issue when you list and to also lower your condition grade to "like new".

CHAPTER 2:
WHAT TO BUY AND
HOW MUCH TO PAY

You now know where to find all the products that you can resell online, but how much should you be paying for all this stuff? If you see an auction of 50 books, what is your maximum bid going to be? How do you know if you will be able to sell everything you are buying so that you are not actually turning your cash into trash?

As a seller, these are the kinds of questions you need to ask yourself every time you are trying to buy items to sell. In this chapter, I am going to give you plenty of tips on what items to buy and how much you should pay for your inventory. The chapter is split into the main product types that I think you should focus on.

I am going to show you what books you should be buying as well as what to look for in CD's, DVD's, and video games. I will also be discussing how to price other miscellaneous items you may come across. I am sure you will find that with my help, and a little bit of experience, you will soon have a trained eye for all those hidden gems just waiting around for you to spot.

Books

When I first started selling online I started by selling used books. Used books are still so underrated and underpriced that it is easy money to sell used books online. If you are just starting out selling used items online I encourage you to focus on the items that are easy to sell and do not require a lot of storage space: Used books, CD's, DVD's, and video games. In particular, I would recommend starting with used books and going from there.

As noted in the prior chapter, you will be able to find used books everywhere. You will almost always run across them at garage sales. In fact, I find my best deals at garage sales. For some reason people value their used books as next to worthless. I can often buy books at $0.25 a book and turn around to sell those books for $5.00 - $10.00 a book.

You will also find tons of books at estate sales, eBay bulk item auctions, library sales, and those police auctions that we discussed earlier. I also love to buy books from the PropertyRoom.com. I can usually pay around $1.00 a book from their auctions and still sell them for around $5.00 - $10.00 a book online. In fact, I have had a number of occasions where I paid $0.25 a book for a box of 30 books and found one or two that were selling for $40.00 and up online. I cannot guarantee you will find that kind of deal in every auction but rest assured, those deals are out there.

Knowing what books to buy and what types of books to focus on is the key to selling those books for an average of $5.00 - $10.00 a book. I break down the types of books into six main categories: mass market paperbacks, mass market hardcovers, trade paperbacks, trade hardcovers, textbooks, and audio books.

1. Mass Market Paperbacks - These are the books to avoid if at all possible. Mass market paperbacks are the small novels you will find in your local supermarket check-out line.

The general size of these books, in inches, is 6.6 x 4.2". Mass market paperbacks are mass produced and typically focus on one type of genre: fiction.

The fact that they are mass produced is the problem with buying these books. There is just too much supply which turns into too many sellers; and once the new book from that author comes out no one wants the old one. I want to show you a quick example of what I mean. I will be using the Amazon.com Marketplace which is a site that I recommend using to sell your items.

If you are near a computer, or the next time you are, go onto Amazon.com and search Hideaway by Dean Koontz. When you do, you will see the paperback book in the search results. Click on it and you will be on that book's product detail page. Next to the book's picture you will see the Amazon.com list price. Below that you will see a link for other sellers. On May 16, 2009 there were 138 used books for sale starting at $0.01.

This book was a #1 national bestseller but to sell it used means selling it for $0.01 on Amazon.com. If you sell it on Amazon.com you will receive $0.01 + $3.99 shipping for a total sale of $4.00. Amazon.com would normally charge you commission of 15% but on $0.01 items there is no commission available to take. There is a variable closing fee of $1.35 and a per-transaction fee of $0.99 (charged if you do not have a Pro Merchant Subscription) that Amazon.com does take. You made a sale of $4.00 and have fees of $2.34 which leaves you with a profit of $1.66 (I will be explaining how to use Amazon.com and their fee structure in detail in the next chapter).

But wait, you still have to ship the book. As of this writing, the rate to ship that particular book is $2.38 through USPS Media Mail which puts you in the red. Plus, you will also have some shipping materials cost (e.g., labels and mailers). Why are there people even selling at $0.01? Well, they have an Amazon Pro Merchant Subscription which means they are not charged the $0.99 per transaction fee. This means that even with a Pro Merchant Subscription you are only going to make $0.27 a book before you deduct your shipping supply cost which might be $0.25. So maybe you are making around $0.03 a sale.

Sounds great, huh? Do not worry, I will show you other ways you can sell those hard to sell books if you get stuck with some of them. After all, in some auctions you will just have them thrown in there and you have to deal with them. If you are a beginner, I just want to warn you about mass market paperbacks. You do not have to waste your time with them and the more selective you are about buying your books the higher your profit margin is going to be. So, for now, I would just stay away from them. In fact, I still try to stay as far away from them as possible.

2. Mass Market Hardcovers – The only type of book that I think is worse than a mass market paperback is a mass market hardcover. The mass market hardcovers are the recent releases from most popular fiction authors such as Dean Koontz, Stephen King, and Danielle Steele. These books are soon converted to the mass market paperbacks. Once that conversion takes place, those hardcovers are literally worthless. Their added weight leads to higher shipping costs and makes it nearly impossible to make any money with them.

How do you spot a mass market hardcover? These are going to be the bigger hardcover books out there. The size of these books is around 9.5 x 6.5". You really want to avoid the fiction novels of this type unless they are a new release. Then, and only then, do I advise buying these books for resale. You have to keep in mind that the bigger the book, the more the shipping cost is going to be. On most of the seller sites you will be listing on, you get a set amount of shipping revenue to use. A typical mass market hardcover is going to weigh around 1.8 lb's. As of this writing, shipping a typical mass market hardcover will cost you $2.77 in postage alone.

Your best bet in dealing with mass market hardcovers is to just look the other way. There are always exceptions to the rule but only if you already know that you can sell that book for a profit. It is much easier if you just focus on the other types of books in order to maximize your profit margin.

3. Trade Paperbacks - These are what I like to call the "money" books. These are typically non-fiction and the size of a trade paperback is around 8.5 x 5.5" or 9 x 6". They are not mass produced like mass market paperbacks and this helps them hold up their resale value. An example is Man's Search for Meaning by Viktor E. Frankl. This is a trade paperback that I purchased for $0.25. On May 16, 2009 this title was selling for $5.50 in "like new" condition. This means that I can sell this title for $5.50 plus $3.99 shipping on Amazon.com for a total of $9.49 before commissions.

As a safety net, you should do just fine buying non-fiction trade paperbacks for around $1.00 - $2.00 each. Of course, always try to buy your books for under $1.00, which is entirely possible.

4. Trade Hardcovers - Trade hardcovers are the bigger brothers of the trade paperbacks. Besides recent textbooks, the non-fiction trade hardcovers are usually going to be the best type of book to sell online. The size of these books is just a bit smaller than the typical mass market hardcover. They are usually 9 x 6".

An example of a trade hardcover is <u>Get Rich with Options</u> by Lee Lowell. If you look that book up on Amazon.com you will see it listed as used for $22.97. I bought this book once for $2.00. If you sold it today on Amazon.com you would get $22.97 plus $3.99 for shipping which comes out to a total of $26.96.

5. Textbooks - Textbooks can be a bit tricky. Their added size and weight mean more shipping costs. However, recent used textbooks can be sold for around $50.00 or more. The key is to try to find textbooks that are recent. If you find a textbook that is an older edition it might be hard to get rid of.

For example, take a look at <u>Biology 8th Edition</u> by Neil A. Campbell and Jane B. Reece on Amazon.com. Used copies are selling for $87.99 as of May 16, 2009. Now look up the 7th edition of that same book and you will see used copies selling for $7.99 as of May 16, 2009. If you have an even older edition is it going to decrease even further in price.

How do you know if it is a recent edition? Check the publication date found in the first few pages of the book. In order to be positive that it is the most recent edition you will most likely have to look up the title using a web enabled cell phone or portable scanner. You will then be able to better judge how much to pay. If you do not have access to a cell phone and the textbook looks old then it is a safe bet to not bother with it. If it is published in the same year or the year before you should consider picking it up but still keep the price you pay low: average $1.00 - $2.00 unless you actually know the value you can resell the book for.

6. Audio Books - You should always be on the lookout for recent audio books on CD. The audio books on tapes still have some value and if you buy them below $0.50 a piece you should be fine; but the premium items are those newly released audio books on CD.

Older audio books on CD can go either way. Most audio books come on five or more CD's. This means the item weighs more than just a typical music CD. The extra weight is going to eat into your total profit in the way of extra shipping costs. If it is an older audio book on CD, and you do not have an idea of the resale value, try to limit the purchase to $1.00 - $2.00. You should be able to sell older audio CD's at an average of $5.00 a piece.

When you are buying audio books on CD just be sure to inspect the CD. If it is completely scratched you will not be able to sell it, or if you do sell it you will most likely get bad feedback from the buyer.

Now that you know the basic book types and sizes to actually look for you can better hone in on them in your searches. Besides the basic book sizes, there are also a few different categories of books that are more profitable to sell than others. The main categories are fiction and non-fiction. For the most part, fiction sells for less than non-fiction. If you are selective in your purchases, you will find that non-fiction books will generally sell anywhere from $5.00 - $10.00 a book. This price includes the book price plus any shipping credit.

Within the main categories of fiction and non-fiction there are some different sub-categories to look for.

Fiction

Fiction can be broken up into the different reading classes and categories. There are children's books, young adults, and adults. Some categories are horror, suspense, mystery, and romance, just to name a few. As a general rule each category is just as bad as the next. New fiction is going to sell well and the fiction in trade paperback form is going to give you a better profit than the mass market paperback form.

Romance novels are the worst of the worst. I will just say there is no love-lost between me and romance novels; my advice is to just end the relationship before it even begins and focus on other book categories.

Along with trade paperback fiction, I have found that certain children's books can give you a fairly decent profit. I would keep purchases of children's books to around $0.50 or less a book. Of course, if you know the value of the book, and the seller is not willing to budge at $0.50 - $1.00, you can raise your price as much as your profit margin allows. You should be safe buying trade paperbacks at $1.00 - $2.00 but always try to buy books for less than $1.00. This is entirely possible, especially at garage and estate sales.

Non-Fiction

There are many categories of non-fiction. Examples are politics, history, biographies, self-help, how-to, philosophy, cookbooks, and I could go on and on. The key thing to remember with non-fiction is that it is better than fiction.

One category in non-fiction to look out for is investment and trading books. Investment and trading books usually come in the trade hardcover format and their resale value holds up surprisingly well. The only thing to watch out for with investment books is a book that is tailored to a specific time. For example, there are mutual fund guides released every year and no one is going to want to read what the best mutual funds to pick are in the year 2000 when it is 2009.

Overall, I think all the major categories of non-fiction are worth taking a close look at and if you focused all your efforts on non-fiction you should have no problem turning a decent profit.

Rare and Collectible Books

The only other book category worth mentioning is rare or collectible books. These are difficult to value unless you know the specific titles. If you do find a very rare, collectible book you probably do not want to list it on Amazon.com or eBay; rather, you would want to find an antique book dealer. I typically will deal in the standard books I know I can sell and sell fast. For further reading on how to value rare books try Antique Trader Book Collector's Price Guide by Richard Russell. You can also go to www.fadedgiant.net. They have a guide to rare and old book values. You can also use their database to search your title's value to see if it truly is a rare find. Another site I recommend is http://rarebookfinds.com. This site also includes further information on rare books and how to value them.

A Final Word on What Books to Avoid

Besides mass market paperbacks and mass market hardcovers there are a few more types of books that you should avoid at all costs. For one, you should avoid all dictionaries and encyclopedias. Keep in mind that if it is a big, bulky, heavy book, like a dictionary, you are going to have to pay more in shipping; you need to know that you can sell that item over your shipping costs to be profitable. You should also steer clear of Bibles, unless it is a specialized or limited edition Bible. So, if you think a Bible has some value look it up online before you commit to a purchase.

CD's, DVD's, and Video Games

I think most people are surprised when I tell them that I actually make more money selling used books than selling CD's, DVD's, and video games. The fact is most people value used books for next to nothing but still try to sell their used DVD's at $5.00 or more. Strangely enough, I can sell a used book for the same, if not more, than a used DVD.

The thing I like about selling CD's, DVD's and video games is that their cost of shipping is less than the cost of shipping a book. They weigh about half a pound which means I can ship it for less and ship it as First Class Mail which delivers faster than Media Mail (which is the most economical way to ship books). This means more happy customers and better feed-back due to fast shipping.

You can apply the same general rules to CD's, DVD's, and video games as you can with books. Of these three categories you will be able to purchase video games for more because you will find that you can easily resell video games for around $10.00 per game. You should be able to sell most CD's and DVD's for around $5.00 per item. Of course, there are plenty that fall under that $5.00 mark.

CD's

Much like with DVD's, not all CD's hold much resale value on the open market. I included audio book CD's in the book section and once again, if you see a recent audio book on CD you should gobble it up. Try to buy those around $2.00 or less if you can. You will usually be able to sell a recent audio book on CD for at least $10.00, if not more.

Music CD's range in value depending on the artist. I find that specialty or lesser known artist's CD's have more resale value than a CD from a well known pop star artist. Take a look on Amazon.com at the resale value of used CD's for an artist like Luciano Pavarotti versus those for an artist like Jessica Simpson. The used Pavarotti CD's sell for at least $10.00 whereas the used Jessica Simpson CD's sell for less than $1.00. Just in case you are unaware, Pavarotti is an opera singer and Jessica Simpson is a pop star.

The key with CD's, as well as DVD's, is to keep your costs low and to be on the lookout for those lesser known titles. Those titles will often be your biggest profits. Of course, if you see recent releases do not be afraid to make a decent offer.

DVD's

The same general rules that I use with books also applies to DVD's. You can split DVD's into two main categories: You have your fiction and your non-fiction. Fiction would be most of the movies you will find in the theatres and non-fiction would be documentaries and how-to videos. The documentaries and how-to videos sell for more than the fiction DVD's.

So, just as with books, you should be on the lookout for those non-fiction or documentary DVD's. You should also still try to limit your price to $1.00 - $2.00 per item until you have some more experience or unless you have a web enabled cell phone that will let you find the actual value of the DVD's.

VHS tapes still do sell but try to buy those for $0.25 or less. If you come across them at garage sales you can easily talk the seller into selling these things for next to nothing because most people already figure that no one would want them.

Video Games

Video games are great items to look for. The resale value holds up fairly well and they are easy to ship. The easiest titles to sell are for the most recent gaming machines. As of May 2009, the most recent gaming machines are the Nintendo Wii, Playstation 3, and the Xbox 360. If you just stuck to video games on those platforms you can easily sell them for at least $10.00 per title. Of course, recent releases are going to get you closer to $30.00.

You should also look for video games made for computers. Just as with the video games for the gaming machines, you can sell recent computer games for close to $30.00 while older games are going to get you around $10.00.

Games for older video game consoles do still have some value. In fact, there are some games on the older consoles that have stopped being produced. The games are still in limited demand which increases their price. Some of those used games are selling for the same price as when they were originally released. Take a look on Amazon.com at *Legend of Mana* for the Playstation. As of May 16, 2009, this game was selling for a used price of $44.50 when it originally sold new for about the same price.

Legend of Mana is an example of an older game on an older console that is selling for more than most recent games on recent consoles. It is hard to tell if an older title will have this kind of value without checking the price for that title on the web. If you are out at a garage sale and do not have access to the web you are still safe buying older games for the older consoles at $1.00 - $2.00. In fact, since the games are old, the seller will probably have no problem accommodating you at that price. Just be sure to check the quality of the disc for scratches.

If you follow these general rules to buying books, CD's, DVD's, and video games then you are going to have a good start to selling online. When you first start to look for items to sell online just be sure to be selective in your purchases. Experience and following the tips in this book are going to help you weed through the trash so you will not be loaded up with junk inventory that will never sell.

Other Items

You can also make money buying miscellaneous items and selling them online. These items include TV's, DVD players, and even furniture. Before you go out and buy everything at that next garage sale, make sure you know the value of the items before you buy them.

Some colleagues of mine will buy broken electronics, fix them, and then sell them online. You could also refurbish furniture and sell that if you have a skill set in that particular area. Your best bet is to have a web enabled cell phone. If you see a DVD player you will need to know what that type of DVD player is going to sell for before you can make an educated offer.

When you sell items other than books, CD's, DVD's, and video games online your best bet is to use eBay. I will be discussing how to sell these miscellaneous items on eBay in the next chapter. For the most part, it is easier to focus your efforts on the same products as I do. You will find the items sell faster and are easier to ship. In addition, if you are planning on starting a home-based business the perfect products are books, CD's, DVD's and video games. They only take up a little space and require no knowledge to refurbish or fix.

That being said, there are still deals to be made in just about any category. I will be showing you how to use eBay to sell anything from electronic devices, to kitchen supplies, to washing machines.

Pre-Order Reports

Before you head out to search for deals or surf the web for items to sell, you can take a look at what items are in high demand. If you have a seller account with Amazon.com (It is free and I will show you how to get it in the next chapter) you can download pre-order reports. Pre-order reports list used items that have been requested by buyers on Amazon.com. You can download the reports for books, music, DVD's, VHS, Camera & Photo, Electronics, Kitchen, Tools & Hardware, and Video Games. The current link to downloading those reports is: https://sellercentral.amazon.com/gp/SDPSupport/preorder-report-US.html/.

If the link has been changed or does not work you can always sign into your seller account, click on the help button on the top right of the screen, and search for "pre-order reports". That should bring you to the page where you will find the link to download reports for the specific categories. These reports are great to have. They will give you an idea of what items are in high demand and what prices buyers are willing to pay for them.

Scanners

The most accurate way to get pricing information while you are in the field is with the use of a barcode scanning system. This is not necessary if you are just starting out because, if you follow my guidelines and are selective in your purchases, you should still be able to turn a decent profit without one. However, if you find you want to take your business to the next level a scanner is the ideal solution.

Scanners work best at all the garage sales, yard sales, thrift stores, used book stores, estate sales, and library sales you will be going to; basically, any venue where you can physically inspect each item before you make your purchase. You will find that most of the auctions will not allow you to physically go through each book or item. You will get an idea of what is in the auction but you will not always have the luxury of pricing each item individually.

Of course, to use a scanner the item needs to have a barcode. The good thing is that everything I am recommending you sell in this book should have a barcode. Barcodes can usually be found on the lower right of the back of any book, CD case, DVD case, or video game case. If you only see a DVD disc but no case then you will not have the barcode and will have to search it online by the product's name.

Portable scanners can be expensive so I advise you to wait until you are serious about moving forward with your business before you make any purchases. There are also scanners that will fit onto most web enabled cell phones. This means you can scan right from your phone and find pricing information on sites like Amazon.com.

There are a number of companies that sell scanners. I recommend looking into:
www.scoutpal.com
www.mediascouter.com
www.asellertool.com.
You can also search www.ebay.com for used scanners.

CHAPTER 3:
LISTING YOUR ITEMS

You have now gone through all of your books, CD's, DVD's, video games, and other junk or have bought some things to sell using my guidelines. The next step is to actually put your items up for sale. The best thing about selling online in today's market is that you no longer need your own website; you do not have to worry about website design, registering your domain name, or processing credit card transactions. There are a number of great websites of established and popular companies where you can sell your stuff; better yet, those companies take care of all the payment processing. I am going to walk you through selling on the five main websites that I think are the best and easiest to use: Amazon.com, Half.com, Alibris.com, Abebooks.com, and eBay.com.

The items that you are trying to sell and your seller type are going to influence which site you should use and how you should use it. Most of the sites allow you to list your items free of charge; you will only be charged a commission if your item sells. Some sites charge you a monthly fee and some allow you to upgrade your service to a monthly fee in order to pay less commission for each sale. Your seller type will also determine if you are going to be selling a high enough volume of items to necessitate a monthly subscription.

Bulk Sales

If you are just trying to sell your junk in order to clear out some space then you have a couple of great options. One is to sell all your like items in bulk; this is going to be the fastest way for you to get rid of your stuff and still make some money. You will make a little less than if you sell item by item but you will be done in a matter of weeks.

If you choose to go this route the first thing you need to do is to separate your books, CD's, DVD's, and video games from your other items. There are some great websites that can help you out here. Companies will buy your used stuff, most will pay for the shipping as well, and then resell it themselves. I recommend the following companies for bulk sales:

Abebooks.com - www.abebooks.com

Abebooks.com is a company that will buy your used books in bulk. You just go to http:/buyback.abebooks.com and enter the books you have for sale. They will then give you a quote and if you accept it you can send them your books and they will send you a check. They will pay the cost of shipping so you do not have to worry about that. Abebooks.com is a site that also allows you to sell your items individually and I will be discussing that part of their website later on in the chapter.

Cash 4 Books - www.cash4books.net

This is a great website for selling your used books in bulk. You simply log onto the website and enter all of your book's ISBN's (International Standard Book Number). A book's ISBN is typically located on the back just above the barcode.

Once you enter all your ISBN's they will give you a price. If you are ok with that amount then you will be able to print shipping labels right from your computer and send them your books. The great thing is that they will pay for shipping.

eCampus.com - www.ecampus.com

This site works similar to cash4books.net and is only for books. You just need to enter your ISBN's to receive an offer. If you accept the offer then you can send them your books and receive a check. They will also pay for the shipping.

DVD Pawn - www.dvdpawn.com

If you have a lot of DVD's, you might consider DVD Pawn. The site works similar to the previously mentioned sites. The submission process is a little different, but not too much. You give them the names of your titles and they will send you an e-mailed quote. You can then ship your DVD's to them and get paid. This site also purchases video games.

Sell My DVD's - www.sellmydvds.com

Just like DVD Pawn, Sell My DVD's focuses on purchasing used DVD's and video games. I think this site is more user friendly than DVD Pawn's. The process is basically the same; enter your titles, get your quote, and ship your stuff.

SecondSpin.com - www.secondspin.com

SecondSpin.com focuses on used CD's but they also purchase used DVD's and video games. Once you are on their site, you simply enter all the UPC's of everything you are trying to sell. The UPC is the number that is under the barcode; it is usually found on the right side of the bottom-back of most items.

Cash For CD's - www.cashforcds.com

Cash for CD's is another great site for selling your used CD's, DVD's, and video games. Their site works the same as the others. The great thing about having a few different companies that do the same thing is that they are in competition to get your stuff; feel free to get quotes from all of them and see who gives you the best offer.

eBay – www.ebay.com

If you have a bunch of items that do not fit into any of the above categories then you can still sell your items on eBay.com. In fact, you will be able to bulk list all your books, CD's, DVD's, and video games too. This method is going to require a little bit more work from you but you should be able to make more money by doing so. In order to sell on eBay you will need an eBay account and you will have to create your own listing. I will be discussing eBay in detail later on in this chapter; you can then use the techniques discussed to create a listing for your bulk items.

Individual Sales

You can make the most money from your items by selling them as individual items. This is how you are going to set up your part-time business (or full-time once you get the hang of it). The home-based business works best if you focus on books, CD's, DVD's, and video games so I am going to focus on those categories. However, I will be telling you how you can make money selling any type of item that you come across as well.

Amazon.com – www.amazon.com

Amazon.com is one of the largest internet retailers out there. Their site is also the easiest to use website for selling your used items. Your stuff is going to sell the fastest when you put it on Amazon.com. However, they currently charge some of the highest commissions which means that you are paying a premium to sell on their site. The premium is well deserved!

Amazon.com has grown like few companies could even dream of. For the year of 1999, Amazon.com had gross sales of $1.6 billion dollars.(2) For the year of 2008, Amazon.com had gross sales of $19.16 billion dollars.(2) Millions of consumers visit their website on a daily basis and now you can take full advantage by making your products seen on their site.

There are two main types of seller accounts on Amazon.com that I will be discussing. There is a Standard Seller account. This account is free to set up and there are no monthly charges. You are only charged a commission on the items you sell. There is also a Pro Merchant account which has the benefit of a lower commission rate but requires a monthly subscription of $39.99.

To set up a Standard Seller account on Amazon.com just go to their website: www.amazon.com. You will first have to register on Amazon.com. This simply requires you to have a valid e-mail address. Once registered you can click on the "your account" link on the top right of the home page or scroll to the bottom of the page and you should see a "sell on Amazon" link.

In order to activate your seller account, you will need to give Amazon.com your bank account and routing information. This is required since Amazon.com will only pay you through direct deposit to your bank account. Once that is completed, you are ready to start listing and start making some money. Who knew that starting a business could be so easy, huh?

If you are ready to graduate from a Standard Seller account to a Pro Merchant account you only need to log into your seller account and click on "Seller Account Information". This will take you to your seller info, deposit information, and on the bottom of the page, the seller plan section. All you have to do is select "upgrade to Pro Merchant" and you are ready to go. Amazon.com will start charging you a monthly subscription of $39.99 and you will pay less commission per sale.

Take a look at the current fee structure of selling on Amazon.com. The fees listed are as of May 2009 and are subject to change if Amazon.com so desires. You will be able to find the current fees by going to Amazon.com and clicking on the "help" link on the top right. From there follow this thread: Help > Selling at Amazon.com > Getting Paid > Fees and Pricing.

Standard Seller Account Fees

Amazon.com will deduct a commission of 6 to 15 percent of the sales price, a per-transaction fee of $0.99, and a variable closing fee. Table 1-1 is the variable closing fee that Amazon.com will collect from you based on the type of product you sell.

	Domestic Standard	Domestic Expedited	International Standard
Books	$1.35	$1.35	$1.35
Music	$0.80	$0.80	$0.80
Videos (VHS)	$0.80	$0.80	$0.80
DVD's	$0.80	$0.80	$0.80
Video Games	$1.35	$1.35	Not available
Software & Computer Games	$1.35	$1.35	Not available
Electronics	$0.45 + $0.05/lb.	$0.65 + $0.10/lb.	Not available
Camera & Photo	$0.45 + $0.05/lb.	$0.65 + $0.10/lb.	Not available
Tools & Hardware	$0.45 + $0.05/lb.	$0.65 + $0.10/lb.	Not available
Kitchen & Housewares	$0.45 + $0.05/lb.	$0.65 + $0.10/lb.	Not available
Outdoor Living	$0.45 + $0.05/lb.	$0.65 + $0.10/lb.	Not available
Computer	$0.45 + $0.05/lb.	$0.65 + $0.10/lb.	Not available
Sports & Outdoors	$0.45 + $0.05/lb.	$0.65 + $0.10/lb.	Not available
Cell phones and accessories	$0.45 + $0.05/lb.	$0.65 + $0.10/lb.	Not available
Musical Instruments	$0.45 + $0.05/lb.	$0.65 + $0.10/lb.	Not available
Office Products	$0.45 + $0.05/lb.	$0.65 + $0.10/lb.	Not available
Toy & Baby	$0.45 + $0.05/lb.	$0.65 + $0.10/lb.	Not available
Everything Else	$0.45 + $0.05/lb	$0.65 + $0.10/lb.	Not available

Table 1-1 (3)

As noted, Amazon.com will also deduct a commission of 6 to 15 percent of the sales price. The percentage of commission charged depends on the type of product being sold. Table

1-2 shows the current commission percentage rates as of May 2009.

Amazon Kindle	15%
Automotive Parts and accessories	12%
Camera and photo	8%
Cell Phones and accessories	15%
Computers	6%
Electronic items	8%
Items in the Everything Else store	15%
Musical Instruments	12%
Watches	13%
All other product lines	15%

Table 1-2 (3)

Now that you know the commission structure of a Standard Seller account you can calculate how much commission would be deducted from a standard book sale. If you sell a book for $5.00 on a Standard Seller account, Amazon.com would charge you a variable closing cost of $1.35, a $0.99 transaction fee, and a $0.75, 15% commission for a grand total of $3.09. This means that you are left with $1.91. Seems as if it would be hard to make money this way, huh?

It all works out because as Amazon.com takes, Amazon.com also gives. They will give you a certain amount of money to ship the product you are selling. Being able to make money on shipping an item is a key to high volume selling online.

This next table (1-3) will show you how much you will receive per sale as shipping credit depending on the type of product you are selling.

	Domestic Standard	Domestic Expedited	International Standard
Books	$3.99	$6.99	$12.49
Music	$2.98	$5.19	$6.89
Videos (VHS)	$2.98	$5.19	$12.29
DVD's	$2.98	$5.19	$12.29
Video Games	$3.99	$6.99	Not available
Software & Computer Games	$3.99	$6.99	Not available
Electronics	$4.49 + $0.50/lb.	$6.49 + $0.99/lb.	Not available
Camera & Photo	$4.49 + $0.50/lb.	$6.49 + $0.99/lb.	Not available
Tools & Hardware	$4.49 + $0.50/lb.	$6.49 + $0.99/lb.	Not available
Kitchen & Housewares	$4.49 + $0.50/lb.	$6.49 + $0.99/lb.	Not available
Outdoor Living	$4.49 + $0.50/lb.	$6.49 + $0.99/lb.	Not available
Computer	$4.49 + $0.50/lb.	$6.49 + $0.99/lb.	Not available
Sports & Outdoors	$4.49 + $0.50/lb.	$6.49 + $0.99/lb.	Not available
Cell phones and accessories	$4.49 + $0.50/lb.	$6.49 + $0.99/lb.	Not available
Musical Instruments	$4.49 + $0.50/lb.	$6.49 + $0.99/lb.	Not available
Office Products	$4.49 + $0.50/lb.	$6.49 + $0.99/lb.	Not available
Toy & Baby	$4.49 + $0.50/lb.	$6.49 + $0.99/lb.	Not available
Everything Else	$4.49 + $0.50/lb.	$6.49 + $0.99/lb.	Not available

Table 1-3 (4)

In our example of selling a $5.00 book, you are left with $1.91 after commissions but Amazon.com will give you $3.99 to ship that book. The amount that will be deposited to your bank account will be $5.90.

Pro Merchant Seller Account Fees

The only commission difference between a Standard Seller account and the Pro Merchant account is the $0.99 per transaction fee. If you sign up as a Pro Merchant the $0.99 per transaction fee is waived but you are paying $39.99 as a monthly subscription. There is no subscription fee required to be a Standard Seller.

When does it make sense to sign up as a Pro Merchant? You need to be selling over 40 items a month for it to be economical for you to sign up. Once you sell your 40th item in the month you have made up the cost of your subscription by having the per transaction fee waived. If you plan to sell only a few items here and there just stick to the Standard Seller account and have fun.

One of the non-commission differences between a Standard and Pro Merchant account is that a Pro Merchant can submit a product detail page to Amazon.com. If Amazon.com does not currently have a product page for the item you are trying to sell then you can go ahead and create one for them. This enables you to list items that were not originally on their website.

Listing on Amazon.com

Once you are signed up with either a Standard Seller account or a Pro Merchant account you are ready to start listing. Two things that I love about listing on Amazon.com are the simplicity and how fast items can sell after being listed. You can list any type of product that you are trying to sell and the process for listing different products is the same. I think Amazon.com is the best site to sell what I like to think of as my main moneymakers: books, CD's, DVD's, and video games.

Before listing, I want to make sure you know where your listing is going to appear. Take a look at any product on

Amazon.com. As an example, I am going to use the book <u>Anatomy of the Bear</u> by Russell Napier. If you search that title on Amazon.com you should see it on the top of the search results. Next to the "buy new" price you will see "31 used & new from $24.16". When you list an item, you will be part of that "31 used & new from $24.16". The actual number of used and new copies available and low price will be different by the time you read this book and enter that search. The thing to note is that when you list on Amazon.com buyers have access to your used or new item from the main search page.

When you click the actual "used & new" link you will be taken to the detail page where you can buy from other sellers. You can filter the results by new, used, and collectible. The main information that buyers can see about the sellers is the condition of the item being sold, seller name, feedback rating, where the product ships from, and a description as to the quality of the item.

Now you know where your product is going to be seen. The key is to be on the top of whatever condition of item you have: new, used, or collectible. No one wants to scroll through pages of sellers because the further they go from page one, the higher they are going to pay since the results are sorted by price.

You have a couple of different choices of how to go about listing your product on Amazon.com. If you go to any product's detail page on Amazon.com you will see a link on the right side of the webpage to "sell yours here". Simply click that link and you will be taken to the first page of the listing process. On this page you need to select the condition of the product: New, Used - Like New, Used - Very Good, Used - Good, Used - Acceptable, Collectible. You will also be able to write a short description of the item. This is where you need to specify if there is anything wrong with the item you are selling and also a great chance to communicate with the buyer; this little window is all the initial communication you have with a buyer and it can be used to set you apart from all the other listings out there.

Keep your descriptions as short as possible and try to stress either your reputation (if you have great feedback) or that you ship orders daily. I do recommend that you ship out your orders daily; in fact, the best way to get good feedback on Amazon.com is through your shipping speed. Amazon.com requires all sellers to ship their orders no more than two business days after the order is received.

The next page of the listing process is where you enter your price and quantity. A window on the right of the screen will show you the lowest new, used, and collectible price. It is a good idea to actually check into the low price when listing if at all possible. Sometimes unscrupulous sellers will sell an item that is similar but not exactly the same as the item they are listing under. They will then set an abnormally low price and try to explain in their description that the item they are selling is not really the item displayed. This happens all the time with textbooks. If the new edition is the 8th edition you will see some people trying to sell the 6th edition under the 8th edition. They will describe the book as the 6th edition and set a low price. However, if you have the 8th edition you can set your price above theirs; but just looking at the low price window does not notify you if there is a big discrepancy between the lowest price and the next lowest price.

Selling a product that is similar to but not exactly the same product described on the product detail page is a practice that is against the Amazon.com community guidelines and those sellers can have their account closed for listing violations. If you see that occurring you can notify Amazon.com of the problem by reporting a community rules violation, which is found in the help section of your seller account.

The third page of the listing process is a confirmation page. You can review your listing and make sure it is correct. You will also see the total commission Amazon.com will charge if the item sells and the total you will make on the sale. Once you confirm your listing it will show up in your inventory in your seller account and should show up live on Amazon.com within 15 minutes.

You can also list items by going directly to your seller account. Log onto Amazon.com, click "Your Account" on the top right, and then click "Your Seller Account" on the right of the screen. This will take you to your seller account homepage. You can view your feedback, get help on selling from Amazon.com, manage your inventory, view orders, and more.

Under the "Manage Your Inventory" section you will see a link to list single items and upload multiple items. The "list single items" link will take you through the same process just described. The "upload multiple items" is there for high volume sellers. You can download a template file from Amazon.com in Excel format. You enter in all your product information for each listing and then you upload one file into Amazon.com. Amazon.com will then create listings for each product so you do not have to manually go through the entire listing process for each item. This can save you a considerable amount of time but you must have an idea as to the selling price of each item you upload. To get around this problem, you can upload inventory in bulk and then go to the "manage your inventory" section of your seller account. Click on "view your current inventory" and you can see if you have the lowest price for each item and what the lowest price is if you do not have it.

Another way to list items is to use an automation program. There are programs that will allow you to scan in your items and then those items will be listed on any number of websites that you choose. Most of those programs require a monthly subscription but they can save a considerable amount of time for high volume sellers. I will be discussing some of these programs in Chapter 7: Automation.

Grading Your Products, Pricing, and Shipping

One of the keys to selling online is feedback. You can get feedback on Amazon.com by providing an honest description of your product and shipping the product out as soon as possible. Your feedback score is one of the few pieces of information that buyers will see about you when they are looking at your item. The highest you can be rated on Amazon.com is five stars. Just think, if a buyer sees the same product at the same price do you think they would buy from someone with a four star rating or five star?

As mentioned before, when you price your items you need to be listed near the top of that first page if you want to sell your items quickly. Unless you have a collector's edition or there is something unique about your item, just list it as low as you can for the condition of your item. When I list a group of random products I price them at the low end, if not the lowest, of same conditioned items. I sell, on average, about 10 - 15 percent of the items that I list within two days; so, be prepared to ship once you list. In fact, I have had many items sell within an hour of listing them on Amazon.com. Amazon.com does let you see the actual sales rank of the item on the item's detail page as well as on the page where you fill out your listing information. The higher the sales rank, the greater the chance the item is going to sell quickly.

The following are the grading conditions for the major categories of product that I recommend selling on Amazon.com. You can find this information by going to your seller account, clicking "seller help" on the top right and then follow this thread on the left: listing > condition guidelines. You will be able to see the required condition guidelines for all the products you can sell on Amazon.com in addition to the ones listed here.

Grading Conditions for Books

- *New*: Just like it sounds. A brand-new, unused, unread copy in perfect condition.
- *Like New*: An apparently unread copy in perfect condition. Dust cover is intact, with no nicks or tears. Spine has no signs of creasing. Pages are clean and are not marred by notes or folds of any kind. Book may contain a remainder mark on an outside edge but this should be noted in listing comments.

- *Very Good*: A copy that has been read, but remains in excellent condition. Pages are intact and are not marred by notes or highlighting. The spine remains undamaged.
- *Good*: A copy that has been read, but remains in clean condition. All pages are intact, and the cover is intact (including dust cover, if applicable). The spine may show signs of wear. Pages can include limited notes and highlighting, and the copy can include "From the library of" labels.
- *Acceptable*: A readable copy. All pages are intact, and the cover is intact (the dust cover may be missing). Pages can include considerable notes--in pen or highlighter--but the notes cannot obscure the text.
- *Unacceptable*: Moldy, badly stained, or unclean copies are not acceptable, nor are copies with missing pages or obscured text. Books that are distributed for promotional use only are prohibited. This includes advance reading copies (ARCs) and uncorrected proof copies. (5)

Grading Conditions for CD's

- *New*: Just like it sounds. A brand-new, unused, unopened CD or cassette in perfect condition.
- *Like New*: An apparently unopened CD or cassette in perfect condition (although it may be out of its original wrapping). The jewel case or cassette case has no scratches or scuffing. The liner notes, inclusions, and/or sleeve are in perfect condition. The CD or tape itself is unmarked, with no sign of wear. CD or cassette case may have a remainder cut-out on the spine but this should be noted in listing comments.
- *Very Good*: A well-cared-for CD or cassette that has been listened to, but remains in great condition and plays perfectly. The jewel case/cassette case may show limited signs of wear, as may the liner notes and inclusions.
- *Good*: The CD or cassette plays perfectly but has clear signs of wear. The jewel case or cassette case is undamaged, and original liner notes are in good, unmarked condition. The CD, cassette, or packaging may have identification markings from its owner.
- *Acceptable*: The CD or cassette plays perfectly, but is otherwise the worse for wear. The jewel case or cassette case may be damaged,

and the liner notes may be marked (but remain complete and legible). The CD, cassette, or packaging may have identification markings from its owner.

- *Unacceptable*: Music that is in any way unplayable, scratched, or recorded over is not acceptable, nor are recordings not manufactured by the copyright holder, including recopied media in any form. Additionally, promotional media is prohibited for sale through Amazon Marketplace. (5)

Grading Conditions for DVD's

- *New*: Just like it sounds. A brand-new, unused, unopened video or DVD in perfect condition in its original packaging and with all original packaging materials included.
- *Like New*: An apparently unopened video or DVD in perfect condition (although it may be out of its original wrapping). The box or jewel case is clean and vivid, with no signs of wear. Suitable for presenting as a gift.
- *Very Good*: A well-cared-for video or DVD that has been played, but remains in great condition. The film is complete, without interruption, and does not skip. The jewel case may show limited signs of wear, as may the liner notes.
- *Good*: A video or DVD with clear external signs of wear, but one that continues to play perfectly. The video or DVD may have identification markings from its owner.
- *Acceptable*: A video or DVD with extensive external signs of wear, but one that continues to play perfectly. The box or jewel case may be damaged, and the notes or other inclusions may be marked (but remain complete and legible). The video or DVD may have identification markings from its owner.
- *Unacceptable*: Video or DVD recordings not created by the copyright holder, including recopied media in any form. Additionally, promotional media is prohibited for sale through Amazon Marketplace, as are recordings in which any aspect of the film is missing or obscured. (5)

Grading Conditions for Video Games

- *New*: Just like it sounds. A brand-new, unused, unopened video game in perfect condition in its original packaging and with all original packaging materials included.
- *Like New*: An apparently unopened video game in perfect condition (although it may be out of its original wrapping). The box and item are pristine, with no signs of wear. Suitable for presenting as a gift.
- *Very Good*: A well-cared-for video game that has been played but remains in great condition. The game and its original packaging are complete and slightly worn, but unmarked and undamaged.
- *Good*: The video game shows wear from consistent use, but remains in good condition. There may be clear external signs of wear and damage to the original packaging or instructions, but the game plays perfectly. The video game may have identification markings from its owner.
- *Acceptable*: The video game is fairly worn, but it continues to work perfectly. The box and instructions may be missing or damaged. The video game may have identification markings from its owner. Sellers are required to note whether the box or instructions are missing in the condition notes field for the item.
- *Unacceptable*: Video games that are not playable or are incomplete, including shareware and freeware versions, are unacceptable, as are games not published by the original manufacturer, including recopied media in any form. Promotional media is prohibited for sale through Amazon Marketplace as well. Additionally, video games in which essential accompanying material is missing (this does not necessarily include the box or instructions) are not permitted. (5)

Further Tips on Listing Your Items

Just like the condition guidelines, the following listing advice can be used on any and all of the seller channels I will be discussing. Honestly and effectively describing your items is going to get you sales as well as feedback which, in turn, will further increase your sales over time.

Books. Following the condition guidelines created by Amazon.com is your first step in creating an effective listing. Did you describe all the defects of the book: highlighted pages, creased spine, bent pages, notes written in the pages, ex-library copy, or remainder mark? In addition, have you described all of the book's benefits: clean pages, spine in excellent condition? Have you also described the benefits of buying from you: fast shipping, seller reputation?

CD's, DVD's, and Video Games. Just as with books, be sure to follow the condition guidelines set forth by Amazon.com. Did you describe all the defects to the CD, DVD, or game disc: small scratches to disc, large scratches to disc, not in original case, no insert or cover art, cracks or other damage to jewel case? In addition, have you described all of the benefits: no scratches to disc, ships in original case, includes original inserts/cover art and instructions? Have you also described the benefits of buying from you: fast shipping, excellent seller rating?

If you follow those simple guidelines you are going to do just fine. I also wanted to show you a couple of examples of the wording of some listings. Before you list any item you can also go to that item's detail page and look at the listings of the other sellers. Take a look and see what you think they are doing wrong and what they are doing right; try to incorporate the techniques they are using that you think are most effective.

On most sites, besides eBay, you will not get a lot of space to describe your product. However, you will have enough space to describe exactly what you need: the condition of the product and a little bit about your service. When I have a new item I will create a listing like this: *Brand New Item. Ships same day or next business day.* If that item is a CD or DVD I will also let the buyer know that it is new plus it is still in its original plastic seal.

An example of a listing that falls into the "like new" category for CD's, DVD's, and video games would be: *Disc is in excellent condition, no scratches or defects. Ships in original case with inserts. Ships same day or next business day.* I try to keep my listings short and sweet. I let the buyer know the CD is in near perfect condition and that I will ship their order in a timely manner. For a book I would just make a slight change: *Book is in excellent condition with no defects. Ships same day or next business day.*

I would use the same formula all the way down the listing guidelines. I first list any defects to the condition because I want the buyer to see that first. If the buyer is not going to be satisfied with the condition of the product, I do not want to hide it from him/her because that will most likely turn into negative feedback. After listing any defects, I will list any positives and then my shipping policy.

One further tip about your listing text is to try to create a standard generic listing for each condition grade. This way you do not have to re-type a specialized listing for each item but rather, you can copy and paste your listing into the correct field. This is essential for full-time professional sellers who will be using any of the automated techniques described in Chapter 7.

A generic listing is easy to do for items in the "new" and "like new" categories because there is nothing wrong with those items. However, creating a generic description for items in the "very-good" to "acceptable" condition categories is a challenge since there may be different things wrong with the items at the same grade level. For example, two books may fall into the "good" condition grade but one has highlighting and the other has clean pages but is an ex-library copy. To get around this, create a generic listing template for regular books and one specific for ex-library books. If you do that you will not have to state, "*book may be an ex-library book*" in all your listings of "good" condition grade books as I have seen from other sellers. I placed a generic listing template that I use in Appendix 5. Feel free to use or modify any of the listings to better suite your needs.

Your First Order on Amazon.com

Now that you have listed your items you are bound to start getting some orders. Once your item sells you will receive an e-mail from Amazon.com letting you know which item has sold and how much you have made. You then have to log into your Amazon.com seller account. Click on the "view your orders" link on the right of the screen and you will see all of your orders. From there you can print a packing slip which will contain all the information you need to ship your product. Ship your item and congratulations on your first sale!

Amazon.com Seller Community and Support

You can find great advice from Amazon.com by logging into your seller account and clicking on the "help" button on the top right of the screen. I also recommend that you check out the seller community discussion boards; there you will be able to get involved with the seller community and learn from other sellers as well as ask questions related to your specific situation. The Amazon.com seller community forums can be located at:

http://www.amazonsellercommunity.com/forums.

Half.com – www.half.com

Half.com is a website that specifically caters to books, CD's, DVD's, video games, and video game systems. The site is owned by eBay. Not too long ago there was talk of eBay closing down the site due to poor performance. The Amazon.com Marketplace was getting all the business. I probably would not recommend Half.com if not for recent developments by eBay on how you can use Half.com. When you list on Half.com, if you have an eBay account, Half.com will create a fixed price eBay listing for you. This way you will be listed on Half.com and on eBay; even with this development you are not going to sell items as fast on Half.com as you would on Amazon.com. The good news is that you can actually make more per item by sell-ing on Half.com.

Half.com uses a tiered commission structure based on the sales price of the item. There is no monthly fee, no variable closing cost, and no transaction fee. They give you a little less shipping credit than Amazon.com but the lack of fees more than makes up for this difference. Table 1-4 is the tiered com-mission structure as of May 2009 and table 1-5 is the shipping credit you will receive if you sell on Half.com.

Selling Price	Half.com Commission
$0.75 - $50.00	15.0%
$50.01 - $100.00	12.5%
$100.01 - $250.00	10.0%
$250.01 - $500.00	7.5%
> $500.00	5.0%

Table 1-4 (6)

Item	USPS Media Mail	Expedited Method
Hardcover Book	$3.07	$5.24
Paperback Book	$2.64	$5.20
Audio Books	$2.64	$5.20
Music	$2.39	$5.20
VHS Movies	$2.14	$5.20
DVD Movies	$2.39	$5.20
Games	$2.89	$5.20
Game Systems	**Ground**	**Expedited Method**
Large Consoles	$13.50	$18.00
Small Consoles	$7.00	$9.00
Controllers	$7.00	$9.00
Flash Cards	$4.00	$6.00
Other Accessories	$5.25	$7.00

Table 1-5 (7)

Signing up as a seller on Half.com is almost the same as Amazon.com. Just go to www.half.com and click on the "sell my stuff" link on the top right. You will then be instructed to create an account, which means submitting your bank information since they also pay you via direct deposit. If you already have an eBay account then you are already registered and can use that same eBay account e-mail and password to log into Half.com.

Listing is also very similar to Amazon.com. Simply look up the item you are selling, grade and price your item, and it should appear live within 15 minutes or so. In order for your item to also appear on eBay you will need to have an eBay account and a PayPal account. If you do not have either, they are simple to sign up for. All you have to do is click on the link provided by Half.com and you will have an eBay and PayPal account set up within minutes.

Once an item is sold, you will go through the same process as Amazon.com. You will get an e-mail confirmation and then you can log into your Half.com account and print the packing slip. The next step is to ship your item. Half.com also prompts you to mark your item as shipped which notifies the buyer that their item is on the way.

The one aggravating thing about dual listing on Half.com and eBay is that your money is split into two holding areas. Items sold on Half.com will be direct deposited based on Half.com's schedule into your bank account. Items sold on eBay are going to be held in your PayPal account until you specify those funds to be deposited to your bank account. In a sense you have to keep track of both accounts to make sure your money is getting deposited to your bank account.

The only other issue I have with Half.com is that items do not sell as fast as when I list them on Amazon.com. However, of all the sites that I list on, I now rank Half.com as the second best in selling used books, DVD's, CD's, and video games. After all, it is free to list and easy to use.

Half.com Support

You can find Half.com seller support information by going to:
http://pages.half.ebay.com/help/index.html.

Alibris – www.alibris.com

Alibris is another seller site that I would recommend looking into. The company does not offer a free type of seller account such as Amazon.com or Half.com. Alibris uses a slightly different fee and commission schedule. However, there are some interesting programs that you can use on Alibris so I do recommend looking into them, although I think you should stick with Amazon.com and Half.com when you are first starting out.

You can sell books, CD's, and DVD's on Alibris. Listing your items is just about the same as with Amazon.com and Half.com. You can use the same grading conditions as listed in the Amazon.com section.

There are two types of seller accounts on Alibris.com: Alibris Basic and Alibris Gold. Alibris Basic is setup for your casual seller while Alibris Gold would be for your professional seller.

Alibris Basic

Alibris charges a $1.00 per transaction fee as well as a 15 percent commission on the item sales price. In addition to that, there is an annual fee of $19.99. You will receive almost the same amount of shipping credit as you would on Amazon.com.

Shipping Credit To Contiguous U.S. Addresses

Shipping Method	Delivery Estimate	First Item Charged	Each Additional Item
Standard	4-14 Days	Books: $3.99 Music & Movies: $2.99	Books $2.19 Music & Movies: $1.99

Expedited	3-8 Days	Books: $6.99 Music & Movies: $5.19	Books: $2.99 Music & Movies: $2.99

Table 1-6 (8)

Shipping Credit To Alaska, Hawaii, U.S. protectorate, P.O. Box, and APO/FPO addresses

Shipping Method	Delivery Estimate	First Item Charged	Each Additional Item
Standard	4-28 Days	Books: $3.99 Music & Movies: $2.99	Books $2.19 Music & Movies: $1.99
Expedited	3-8 Days	Books: $6.99 Music & Movies: $5.19	Books: $2.99 Music & Movies: $2.99

Table 1-7 (8)

Alibris Gold

  The Alibris Gold program has a different fee structure. The $1.00 per transaction fee will be waived. You will still be charged 15 percent of the item sales price and you will be charged a monthly fee similar to the Amazon Pro Merchant account. The monthly fee is tiered as to how many item listings you have per month. Table 1-8 is the flat monthly fee structure for Alibris Gold members as of May 2009.

Average listing per month	Flat monthly fee
0-500	$9.95
501-1,000	$15.00
1,001-2,000	$20.00
2,001-4,000	$30.00
4,001-10,000	$35.00
10,001-20,000	$40.00
20,001-30,000	$60.00
30,001-50,000	$90.00
50,001-100,000	$125.00
100,001-250,000	$150.00
250,001-500,000	$250.00
500,001-1,000,000	$350.00
1,000,001 +	$450.00

Table 1-8 (9)

The benefits of the Alibris Gold program are the software upgrades that are available to you. You will have access to re-pricing software, inventory management, and automated order data. If you go to www.alibris.com/sellers/program-fees you will see a layout of the differences between the two programs.

Both the Alibris Basic and the Alibris Gold allow you to take part in their partner sales channels. You need to be a member of most of those sales channels in order to take part in this program. The partner sales channels include: Amazon.com, Barnes & Noble.com, Blackwell, Borders, Books-a-Million, Chapters/Indigo, Half.com, and Ingram.

These partnerships allow your product to be listed on those websites once you list on Alibris. The only caveat is that you will pay a slightly higher commission rate depending on the sales channel it is sold on. For example, if the product is sold on Amazon.com you will then pay the 15 percent Amazon.com commission, the Amazon.com variable closing cost, and then a smaller Alibris fee of the greater of 5 percent or $0.25.

Alibris Seller Community and Support

You can access the Alibris seller support website by going to:
http://www.alibris.com/sellers/help.

Alibris also has a forum set up for you to connect with other sellers. You can find the Alibris seller community forum at:
http://www.alibris.com/sellers/forums.

Abebooks.com – www.abebooks.com

Abebooks.com is a great site for booksellers. The site was developed with the bookseller in mind; currently, you can only sell books, including audio books, on their website. Abebooks.com requires a monthly subscription for all types of sellers. The monthly fee is based on the number of books you have listed on their site. Table 1-9 is the monthly fee structure as of May 2009.

Number of Books	Rate per Month
0-500	$25.00
501-4,000	$37.00
4,001-10,000	$42.00
10,001-20,000	$53.00
20,001-30,000	$80.00
30,001-50,000	$125.00
50,001-100,000	$200.00
100,001-150,000	$300.00
150,001-500,000	$400.00
500,001 +	$500.00

Table 1-9 (10)

In addition to the monthly fee, you will be charged a sales commission of 8 percent of the total item amount. This includes the book price plus the shipping charges. On top of that, if it is a credit card order there is an additional 5.5 percent fee. If the payment is made via PayPal, check, or money order then the 5.5 percent fee would not apply; however, you would have a PayPal service fee applied by PayPal.

The best thing about Abebooks.com is that they let you specify your shipping price by a shipping matrix they have and you collect the entire shipping fee. They also provide a free inventory management software called HomeBase. If you are a

professional seller with thousands of books you are going to need some type of software such as HomeBase to keep track of your inventory and keep the headaches to a minimum. You can find the link to HomeBase by going to:
www.abebooks.com/books/homebase/main.shtml.

The flexibility with shipping rates and their low commission structure will help your profit margin, but just as with the other sites, your books will not sell as well as they will on Amazon.com. My advice is to stick with Amazon.com or Half.com at first until your business and inventory start to grow. Once you get the hang of it you should be looking for other sites to list your products on and other ways to improve sales. I will be discussing some automation services later on; these services will be needed if you are looking to become a professional seller. The programs will allow you to list simultaneously on any number of different seller websites, automatically re-price your items, and automate your order management and shipping process.

Abebooks.com Seller Community and Support

You can access the Abebooks.com seller support website by going to:
http://www.abebooks.com/help/help/seller-help-topics.html.

The Abebooks.com seller community forum is located at:
http://forums.abebooks.com.

eBay – www.ebay.com

No book about selling online would be complete without mention of eBay. eBay was founded in 1995 by Pierre Omidyar. As of 2007, the company reported the value of items sold on eBay's platforms was around $60 billion.(11) That number equates to roughly $1,900 worth of items being sold per second on their site.(11) eBay reports that they have about 84 million registered users. eBay is different from the other websites that I have mentioned so far. eBay has built itself up as being an online marketplace focusing on an auction listing format. Unlike the other sales channels, sellers on eBay will typically list a starting price for their item and then a time period for how long the listing will remain active. Buyers then bid on the item until the auction is over; most auctions last three to seven days.

There are a number of different ways that you can use eBay: they have the standard auction format, a fixed price format, and even an eBay Store format. The pricing and listing of items is more complex and time consuming than the other sales channels so I still would advise you to start out with a site like Amazon.com if you are only selling books, CD's, DVD's, and video games. However, if you have other items then you may want to dig deeper into eBay.

It is free to register on eBay; however, if you want to sell anything on eBay you will want to have a PayPal account. Getting a PayPal account is also free as PayPal will only charge you fees if you use them to accept payment. eBay owns PayPal and the relationship between the two is as follows: sellers list their items on eBay, buyers can purchase those items with a credit card or through PayPal, sellers do not have to have their own merchant accounts (which usually require a monthly fee) but can use PayPal, and PayPal will handle all the payment information so sellers do not have to worry about the liabilities associated with handling credit card payments. It is a simple and streamlined process that results in a safe and speedy transaction.

To register with eBay just go to www.ebay.com and sign up. To register with PayPal just go to www.paypal.com and give them the necessary information.

Standard Auction

Once you have your PayPal account and are registered on eBay, you can start listing your products. The most common way to list on eBay is to use their standard auction feature. You will pick the starting price for your item, the shipping cost, and the length of the auction; after that, just sit back and let the bidding begin.

Unlike the other sites I have shown you, eBay charges you to list items. The fees are based on the starting price of the item so it is always best to choose a low starting price. The current fee structure of eBay can be found by going to http://pages.ebay.com/help/sell/fees.html and looking under the category of "Auction Style Listing Fees". To save you some time and to help illustrate my points I have a few tables for you.

Insertion Fees: Auction Style

Starting or Reserve Price	Insertion Fee: Books, Music, DVD's & Movies, Video Games	Insertion Fee (other categories)
$0.01 - $0.99	$0.10	$0.15

$1.00 - $9.99	$0.25	$0.35
$10.00 - $24.99	$0.35	$0.55
$25.00 - $49.99	$1.00	$1.00
$50.00 - $199.99	$2.00	$2.00
$200.00 - $499.99	$3.00	$3.00
$500.00 or more	$4.00	$4.00

Table 1-10 (12)

When you open an auction style listing you will have to pay the insertion fees listed in table 1-10 even if your item does not sell. If the item does sell you will pay the following closing fees which eBay calls, "Final Value Fees":

Final Value Fees: Auction Style

Closing Price	Final Value Fee
Item not sold	No Fee
$0.01 - $25.00	8.75% of the closing value
$25.01 - $1,000.00	8.75% of the initial $25.00 ($2.19), plus 3.5% of the remaining closing value balance ($25.01 - $1,000.00)
Equal to or Over $1000.01	8.75% of the initial $25.00 ($2.19), plus 3.5% of the remaining closing value balance $25.01 - $1,000.00 ($34.12), Plus 1.5% of the remaining closing value balance ($1000.01 - closing value)

Table 1-11 (12)

If you list a DVD on eBay in the auction style format with a starting price of $5.00, you will pay an insertion fee of $0.25. If that item sells for $10.00 you will then pay an additional $0.88 (8.75% of $10.00) final value fee. If you are using PayPal you will also be charged the PayPal transaction fee. The PayPal transaction fee is based on the total sales amount; this includes the item price plus shipping. The eBay fees are just based on the item sales amount. As of May 2009 the PayPal transaction fees were as follows:

PayPal Transaction Fees: Standard Rate

Monthly Sales	Price per Transaction
$0.00 USD - $3,000.00 USD	2.9% + $0.30 USD
$3,001.00 USD - $10,000.00 USD	2.5% + $0.30 USD
$10,000.01 USD - $100,000.USD	2.2% + $0.30 USD
> $100,000.01 USD	1.9% + $0.30 USD

Table 1-12 (13)

If you charged $3.99 for shipping then the total PayPal fee would be calculated by taking $10.00 (Item) + $3.99 (Shipping) = $13.99. Multiply that by 2.9% and add $0.30 and you will have a fee of $0.71. Your combined eBay and PayPal fee would then be $1.84.

eBay's fee structure is a bit more complicated than the other websites I recommend selling on and the tables listed are by no means a complete description of eBay fees. On top of the mandatory fees you can always add things to your individual listing to make it stand out from the rest. Some sellers add listing upgrades called "Feature Fees" to enhance their listings. Feature fees include upgrades such as a border around your listing or shading to your listing to make it stand out. For now, do not get too caught up in extra fees that you may not need but rather, focus on the two main types of eBay listings.

Fixed Price Listing

An alternative to the auction style listing format is to do what is called a fixed price listing. When you create a fixed price listing you are going to create a listing similar to that on Half.com or Amazon.com. There will be no auctioning of your item; the buyer will either accept your price and purchase the item immediately or click away.

The fixed price insertion fee is typically less than what you would pay for an auction style listing. The final value fees are a little bit higher. Tables 1-13 and 1-14 will help shed some light on the fixed price listing fees.

Insertion Fees: Fixed Price

Starting or Reserve Price	Insertion Fee: Books, Music, DVD's & Movies, Video Games	Insertion Fee (other categories)
$1.00 and above	$0.15	$0.35

Table 1-13 (12)

Final Value Fees: Fixed Price

Category	Fee Range	Final Value Fee
	(Item not sold = no fee)	
Consumer Electronics, Video Game Systems, Cameras & Photo	$0.01 - $50.00	8.00% of the closing value
	$50.01 - $1,000.00	8.00% of the initial $50.00, plus 4.50% of the remaining closing value balance ($50.01 - $1000.00)
	Equal to or Over $1000.01	8.00% of the initial $50.00, plus 4.50% of the initial $50.01 - $1,000.00, plus 1% of the remaining closing value balance ($1000.01 - closing value)
Computers & Networking	$0.01 - $50.00	6.00% of the closing value
	$50.01 - $1,000.00	6.00% of the initial $50.00, plus 3.75% of the remaining closing value balance ($50.01 - $1000.00)
	Equal to or Over $1000.01	6.00% of the initial $50.00, plus 3.75% of the initial $50.01 - $1,000.00, plus 1% of the remaining closing value balance ($1000.01

		- closing value)
Clothing, Shoes & Accessories	$0.01 - $50.00	12.00% of the closing value
	$50.01 - $1,000.00	12.00% of the initial $50.00, plus 9.00% of the remaining closing value balance ($50.01 - $1000.00)
	Equal to or Over $1000.01	12.00% of the initial $50.00, plus 9.00% of the initial $50.01 - $1,000.00, plus 2% of the remaining closing value balance ($1000.01 - closing value)
Books, Music, DVD's & Movies, Video Games	$0.01 - $50.00	15.00% of the closing value
	$50.01 - $1,000.00	15.00% of the initial $50.00, plus 5.00% of the remaining closing value balance ($50.01 - $1000.00)
	Equal to or Over $1000.01	15.00% of the initial $50.00, plus 5.00% of the initial $50.01 - $1,000.00, plus 2% of the remaining closing value balance ($1000.01 - closing value)
All other categories	$0.01 - $50.00	12.00% of the closing value
	$50.01 - $1,000.00	12.00% of the initial $50.00, plus 6.00% of the remaining closing value balance ($50.01 - $1000.00)
	Equal to or Over $1000.01	12.00% of the initial $50.00, plus 6.00% of the initial $50.01 - $1,000.00, plus 2% of the remaining closing value balance ($1000.01 - closing value)

Table 1-14 (12)

The standard time duration for a fixed price listing is 30 days. To avoid having to manually relist your item if it does not sell you can also use the "Good 'Til Cancelled" time limit. eBay will then renew your listing every 30 days and you will be charged an insertion fee each time.

As with the auction style listing, you can add feature fees on top of the insertion fees in order to make your listing stand out from the rest. In my experience, it is not always necessary to pay an extra $4.00 to put a border around your listing. When I sell used books I am sometimes only making $4.00, so my listings might look nice and pretty but I would be losing money. The key things that you do want in a listing are the free ones. Make sure you have a picture of your item. Make sure you thoroughly describe your item. Other than that, the other feature fees are just going to eat into your profit margin too much. You can view all the available feature fees by going to http://pages.ebay.com/help/sell/storefees.html.

eBay Store

An alternative to selling an item through a standard auction style listing or a fixed price listing is to open an eBay Store. When you open an eBay Store you will have your own online store right on eBay! The ability to customize your webpage is fairly limited but the fees are quite reasonable.

Opening a store requires you to pay a monthly fee and I would only recommend doing so after you gain some experience selling on eBay as well as on the other major sales channels I have discussed. The store is easy to open and does not require any specific html or webpage building knowledge. Table 1-15 displays the eBay Store monthly fees.

eBay Store Subscription Fees

Store Level	Fee
Basic	$15.95/Month
Premium	$49.95/Month
Anchor	$299.95/Month

Table 1-15 (14)

When you have an eBay Store you can list your items in a store inventory format. The store inventory format is, in a sense, the same as a fixed price listing. The main difference is the fee structure. You save a lot on the insertion fees and you also save on adding feature fees should you choose to do so. The insertion fees for a store inventory format are listed in table 1-16.

eBay Store Insertion Fees

Price	30 days	Good 'Til Cancelled
$1.00 - $24.99	$0.03	$0.03/30 days
$25.00 - $199.99	$0.05	$0.05/30 days
$200.00 and above	$0.10	$0.10/30 days

Table 1-16 (14)

The final value fees are also a little bit different when you sell through the store inventory format.

eBay Store Final Value Fees

Price	Final Value Fee
Item not sold	No Fee
$1.00 - $25.00	12% of the closing price
$25.01 - $100.00	12.00% of the initial $25.00 ($3.00), plus 8% of the remaining closing value balance.
$100.01 - $1,000.00	12.00% of the initial $25.00 ($3.00),

	plus 8.00% of the initial $25.01 - $100.00 ($6.00), plus 4.00% of the remaining closing value balance $100.01 - $1,000.00
Over $1,000.01	12.00% of the initial $25.00 ($3.00), plus 8.00% of the initial $25.01 - $100.00 ($6.00), plus 4.00% of the initial $100.01 - $1,000.00 ($36.00), plus 2% of the remaining closing value balance ($1,000.01 - closing value)

Table 1-17 (14)

The one issue that I have with the eBay Store listing format is that they do not show prominently on the eBay website. When someone searches the title of an item you have in your store inventory, eBay will usually list the items in auction format first, the fixed price format second, and the eBay Store format last. In fact, users typically have to click a link to see more items in eBay Stores. This does not sit well with me as the key to selling anything online is to be "in front" of potential buyers. You will be most successful when you are on the first page of search results. The eBay Store format does not seem to let you do that. In fact, consider the following taken from eBay.com, "Store Inventory listings appear in your Store with other regular auction-style and Fixed Price listings. They also appear in certain circumstances on eBay.com search result pages".(14)

Note that eBay stated, "...in certain circumstances". In other words, you have no way of knowing if your item will show up on the search result pages without having the buyer click on another link to see results in eBay Stores. That is a definite negative to the eBay Store. The plus is that you have your own store and you can try to drive traffic directly to your online storefront. In fact, eBay gives you a store referral credit when you drive traffic to your store.

What Works Best on eBay?

Now that you know the three major types of listings that you can do on eBay, which one works best for your situation? That really depends on what you are selling. If you are selling the items that I recommend then you will do best to place fixed price listings.

The main reason that you want to do a fixed price listing for books, CDs, DVD's, and video games is that it may take longer than the standard auction time of one week to sell an item. You want to list your products on sites that allow you to leave that listing there until it sells. One of the cheapest ways to do this on eBay without having an eBay Store is to create a standard fixed price listing. You can select to have your listing "Good 'Til Cancelled" which means that it will renew every 30 days; of course, you will be charged the insertion fee with each renewal.

However, when you come across a recent release or an item in high demand then you will want to put that in as a standard auction listing. You can check the demand of any item by seeing who else is selling it on eBay. Are people actively bidding on those items? How much are the items selling for? Another way to find out if your item will be in demand is to go to Amazon.com. Look up the item you are going to sell and you will see the Amazon.com sales rank on the item detail page. The sales rank is in the middle of the page below the product details. If you have an item in the top 100 or even top 1,000 then rest assured, you have an item that is in demand.

If you are selling an item in high demand you should focus on creating an auction style listing. This way, you can capitalize on the demand by letting the buyers fight for your item; you will probably make more this way then if you started a high fixed price listing. In addition, an auction style listing provides you with the ability to ship your products when the listing is over (assuming the buyer pays you on time); with a fixed price listing you never know when your item is going to sell.

If you are focusing on selling used books, CD's, DVD's, or video games I would suggest selling on Half.com if you want to get exposure to eBay. Half.com just started a new feature where they will create a fixed price listing for you on eBay when you list your item on Half.com; you just have to be registered with eBay, have a PayPal account, and sign up for the ability to dual list on Half.com. When you do that your listing will show up on Half.com as well as on eBay. If the item sells on eBay you will pay the fixed price final value fees as well as the PayPal transaction fee. If the item sells on Half.com you will pay the Half.com commission rate of 15 percent.

When your item sells through an auction style listing, the buyer may not pay you right away. In fact, just bidding on the item does not require the buyer to guarantee that they will pay. Sometimes (but not often in my experience) the buyer will walk away. This is why you need to wait until you receive payment before you ship an item. If the buyer has not paid in a couple of days you can go into your eBay account and send them a friendly reminder e-mail.

Remember when you list on eBay to include a picture of your product. The good news is that eBay has pictures of most books, CD's, DVD's, video games, and some other products. When you enter your product information, and it matches a picture that eBay has on file, eBay will ask you if you want to include that picture. If you are selling an item that is not yet on file with eBay then you will need to take a picture of that item and upload it into your listing.

You can upload your picture in any number of ways. If you have access to a scanner and your item is flat you can scan an image of it and then upload that right into your listing. If you take a picture of your item make sure it looks professional; nothing will hurt your sales more than a bad picture. The best advice is to set your background on plain white paper; try to avoid laying your products on your kitchen table or your floor. You want buyers to see that you are a professional seller. Just keep your images clean, your descriptions simple and to the point, and you will do just fine on eBay.

Before you get too involved with listing all your stuff on eBay, take a look around the website. Look at items that are in high demand and are actively bid on. Take note of how the other sellers have structured their listings and what their detail pages look like. This will help you prepare a professional listing that will draw in as many bidders as possible.

One thing that sets eBay apart from the other websites that you can sell on is the feedback. On eBay the sellers can also leave feedback on the buyers. This causes both parties to work hard to make sure the transaction is as smooth as possible. eBay users pride themselves in the quantity and quality of their feedback no matter if they are buyers or sellers. As a seller on eBay it is important to routinely go through your shipped orders and leave feedback on all your buyers; this will get you involved in the eBay community and will also encourage your buyers to leave you feedback.

I do recommend that you use eBay when you are selling larger items such as a washer/dryer or refrigerator. When you list a product you can specify that the buyer will have to pick up the item from you so you will not have to pay the shipping cost for a large item. This will reduce your potential number of buyers but, for the most part, you will not be able to make much selling items that would need to be shipped via a freight company because they are too large to ship via UPS or FedEx.

eBay.com Seller Community and Support

eBay has the most extensive seller support help, education, and community services of any of the websites that I have discussed in this book. There are seller discussions, general discussion boards, answer centers, eBay blogs, and even chat rooms. You can view their community services page by going to:
http://hub.ebay.com/community.

eBay has help and support for anyone looking to buy or sell on eBay. The main help and support page for sellers can be found at:
http://pages.ebay.com/help/sell/selling-basics.html.

eBay also offers an eBay University course in selected areas. The eBay University courses are taught by people who have passed a certification course required by eBay. The classes are not free and the fee depends on the teacher. I would say the average cost of a course is $100-$120. You can find courses in your area by going to:

http://pages.ebay.com/university.

CHAPTER 4:
SHIPPING YOUR ORDERS

So far, you have found some stuff to sell, listed those items on one of the recommended websites, and perhaps you just received your first order. Before you start counting your money remember that you still have to find a way to get that item into the hands of your buyer, the quicker the better. You can think of shipping as two parts: Postage and Supplies.

Postage

Shipping items has never been easier; there are a number of shipping programs that allow you to use your computer to print postage right from your own printer. In fact, you do not even need any shipping program as you can take your items directly to the Post Office and pay for your shipments that way. However, if you want to avoid standing in line all day at Post Office you will want to look into some type of shipping program.

Using an online postage company is going to save you a considerable amount of time and is recommended even if you are only going to be selling for a couple of months. Perhaps you are only going to sell your used stuff and then be done with it. Once you are done selling your items you can cancel your shipper account; just be sure to sign up with an account that has a monthly membership.

When shopping around for online postage companies, there are a few things to look out for. If you are selling primarily books, CD's, DVD's, and video games, you are going to want a company that allows you to print Media Mail postage. You are also going to want a service that allows you to hide the postage paid, or in other words print "stealth postage". Stealth postage is important because the buyer might pay $3.99 for shipping but it may have cost you only $2.38 to ship it. If you do not print with stealth postage the actual shipping cost of $2.38 will show up in the right corner of the label printed; this can lead buyers to wonder why they were charged $3.99 when the postage was $2.38. It is best to have the ability to hide the actual amount of postage you paid so you will not end up with customer complaints about the shipping cost.

For the most part, you are going to be shipping with the U.S. Post Office (USPS). USPS is the most economical way to ship when compared to the other major parcel companies, such as UPS, FedEx, and DHL.

Table 1-18 lists the USPS basic domestic shipping rates as of May 2009. Please note that the USPS as of late has not been shy about raising rates. When you establish your shipping account you will be able to take note of any rate increases and factor this increase into your selling practices. In addition, you can log onto www.usps.com/prices to view the current USPS shipping rates.

USPS Shipping Rates: Domestic Prices

Domestic Service	Average Delivery Time	Starting Price	Pricing Factors
Express Mail	Overnight, most locations	From $13.05	Prices based on weight and distance
Priority Mail	1 - 3 days	From $4.95	Prices based on weight and distance

First-Class Mail	1 - 3 days	From $0.44	Prices based on weight and shape
Parcel Post	2 - 9 days	From $4.90	Prices based on weight and distance
Media Mail	2 - 9 days	From $2.38	Prices based on weight

Table 1-18 (15)

As previously mentioned, USPS offers a shipping method called "Media Mail". Media Mail is going to be your shipping method of choice for all books, CD's, DVD's, and video games that weigh eight ounces or more. The reason is that the shipping price for Media Mail is based on weight with no regard to distance. Only certain items can be shipped via Media Mail. The basic restriction is that it has to be media. USPS defines how to use Media Mail on their website: "Media Mail service is a cost effective way to mail books, sound recordings, recorded video tapes, printed music, and recorded computer-readable media (such as CD's, DVD's, and diskettes). Media Mail cannot contain advertising except for incidental announcements of books. The maximum weight for Media Mail is 70 lbs."(16)

There are a few things you should know about Media Mail. First, USPS states that if you send anything via Media Mail your package cannot contain any advertising. The Post Office that I routinely deal with has defined advertising to include requests for feedback.

When you sell an item, whether it is on Amazon.com, Half.com, or eBay you will be able to print an invoice. This invoice will include instructions on how that customer can leave you feedback. This has gotten me in hot water as the Post Office refused to deliver my packages that were shipped via Media Mail because of the instructions on how to leave feedback. The good thing is that I had just starting selling books so I did not have that many orders; I began printing the invoices without the instructions on leaving feedback or just cutting that section off.

Now, I have never found where the USPS defines "advertising" as a request for feedback but you can read the mailing standards and rules for shipping items via Media Mail by going to:

http://pe.usps.gov/text/dmm300/370_cover.htm.

You can also find the entire USPS Domestic Mail manual at:

http://pe.usps.gov/text/dmm300/dmm300_landing.htm.

If the USPS changes those links you can always go to www.USPS.com and do a search for the manual.

The second thing that I think you should know about Media Mail is the delivery time. USPS states that the delivery time for Media Mail is 2 - 9 days. Note at the top of table 1-18 that the delivery time given is listed as "Average Delivery Time". Media Mail can take significantly longer than 2- 9 days; this is especially true when you ship outside the contiguous United States or to a military address. Deliveries to Alaska and Hawaii can actually take 2 - 4 weeks.

Keep that in mind when you have orders shipping outside the contiguous U.S. If possible, send those orders via First-Class Mail. You can only ship an item as First-Class Mail if it is 13 ounces or less. If the item is over that limit, and your profit is large enough, you may want to send the item via Priority Mail or use another shipping service such as UPS or FedEx.

However, most of the time, you will find that Media Mail is going to be the most economical way to ship.

Items less than eight ounces can be shipped for less money than Media Mail and via a faster service: First-Class Mail. Whenever possible you should ship your items First-Class Mail. Doing so will ensure that your shipment reaches the hands of your buyers quickly. After all, shipping speed is one of the major factors that will encourage buyers to leave you feedback.

Online Postage Companies

Endicia - www.endicia.com

Endicia has a great online postage service that allows you to print USPS postage right through you own printer. The set up is simple as you just need to decide on what type of service you want, download the software, and you are ready to go. Endicia has five main account types: Free, Standard, Premium, Professional, and Platinum.

While the Free might sound the best it lacks the shipping services you are going to need. The Free account only allows you to print First-Class, Express, Flat Rate Priority, and International one ounce. At a minimum, you are going to want to go with the Standard account which will allow you to print all the postage types you are going to need. In addition, you will be able to add e-mail shipment notifications, delivery confirmation, buy insurance, and more. The only thing that you will want that the Standard does not have is the ability to print stealth postage.

Since I believe you do need to have the ability to print stealth postage, I would recommend the Premium account. As your business grows you will start to look into the Professional and Platinum accounts as they will enable you to import your orders from your database and help streamline your shipping process.

You can print the postage on standard paper from your printer or on specialized shipping labels. If you are a high volume seller you are probably going to want to look into getting a dedicated thermal printer to print labels. I will discuss the best ways to actually print the postage in the supplies section of this chapter.

The current account rates as of May 2009 are listed in table 1-19.

Account Type	Rate
Endicia Standard	$9.95
Endicia Premium	$15.95
Endicia Professional	$34.95
Platinum Shipper	$99.95

Table 1-19 (17)

The company usually has a free 30 day trial offer that you can take advantage of. In addition, look to see if the company is currently offering any package deals or starter kits. Endicia's pricing is competitive with the other companies out there so you will get your money's worth by trying out the Endicia Premium for $15.95.

Stamps.com - www.stamps.com

Stamps.com offers the same basic features as Endicia's Premium account type. You can print all the postage types you are going to need as well as the ability to print stealth postage. You will also have access to e-mail shipment notifications and delivery confirmations. Stamps.com lacks some of the advanced features found in the Professional and Platinum Shipper accounts of Endicia. You will only need these features if you begin to grow your business and are shipping out hundreds of orders a day; so, in the beginning, either a Stamps.com account or the Endicia Premium account will work just fine for you.

Stamps.com is also a monthly subscription service. Once you sign up you will download the software and you are ready to start shipping. The standard account is listed as starting at $19.99 a month.(18) The special offer as of late includes a free four week trial, free five lb. scale, $5.00 worth of postage, and coupons for $20.00 in postage redeemable after your free trial.

If you choose to go with Stamps.com I would call them after your trial period and ask them to lower the $19.99 fee per month to $15.95. I will not guarantee that they will do this for you but I will say that I know it has happened. After all, Endicia offers the exact same service for $15.95 so there is no reason why they should not accommodate you. This way you will get the same monthly rate as Endicia but also get a free scale! And if they do not want to play ball then just switch to Endicia and according to the current free scale offer, "The scale is a $50.00 value and is yours to keep with no additional obligation".(18) Be sure to read the details of the offer to make sure Stamps.com has not changed the requirements.

Pitney Bowes - www.pitneyworks.com

Pitney Bowes is another online postage service company like Endicia and Stamps.com. The fees for Pitney Bowes are a little different as they require you to commit to a one year rental of the software. They have three different offers priced at $15.99, $18.99, and $21.99. The $18.99 and the $21.99 offers include a 10 lb. and a 30 lb. scale respectively.

I recommend going with Endicia or Stamps.com because you do not have to commit to an account term. Maybe after selling for a month you do not feel it is something you want to keep doing; with Endicia or Stamps.com you can simply close your account but with Pitney Bowes you are stuck paying out the rest of your rental agreement.

Click-N-Ship - www.USPS.com

The Post Office also allows you to print postage from your own printer. The service does not require a monthly subscription but you are only allowed to print Express Mail and Priority Mail for domestic shipments and Global Express Guaranteed, Express Mail International, and Priority Mail International for international shipments.

eBay/PayPal/Half.com

If you are focused on selling through eBay and Half.com you can take advantage of a great program through PayPal. PayPal offers a shipping service that has no monthly fees or surcharges. The caveat is that the order must have been paid through Half.com, PayPal, or eBay.

PayPal's online postage service includes all the goodies that you are going to need: e-mail confirmation, tracking information, Media Mail availability, and even stealth postage. After making a sale on eBay, Half.com, or any payment through PayPal, you can click the "print shipping label" link. You will then be directed to PayPal's shipping center. You will still need a scale to get the exact weight, but other than that you only need to select your service and any other options and you are ready to go.

Another benefit of this service is that you will not have to enter in the shipping address, it will be pre-populated for you. PayPal will also send an automated e-mail to the buyer to let him/her know that their package is on the way. The service is so easy to use that I wish Amazon.com had something similar. Who knows, maybe by the time you read this they will. Either way, this is a great shipping service to use for those that prefer eBay and Half.com.

Shipping Supplies

Now that you know where to find postage, the next step is to find packaging supplies that will allow your product to get to your customers intact and for as little cost to you as possible. The good news is that there are plenty of companies that sell shipping supplies. I will be listing a couple that I have used in this section and more in the Appendix section, but I want to stress that almost any company will do; just be sure to research their prices for the best current deals. In addition, try to pick a company that operates close to where you live. This will decrease the shipping cost you have to pay in order to get your supplies. I like to use a company that has a warehouse a few cities away; most companies allow you to pick up your supplies so you do not have to pay for shipping. In the long run, being able to pick up your supplies can save you big money in shipping costs each year.

You have a number of different shipping supply options available to you and the right supplies depend on what types of products you are going to be shipping. Are you shipping primarily books and DVD's? Or do you have different items of varying size like electronics? If you are just starting out I recommend selling the same categories that I focus on. Doing so will keep your shipping supply cost to a minimum; you will not have to go around trying to buy all different sizes of mailers and boxes.

There are four main ways to ship books, CD's, DVD's, and video games: padded mailers, rigid mailers, corrugated boxes, and easy-fold mailers. The cheapest way to go is usually with padded mailers. Padded mailers are large envelopes that are lined with bubble wrap. Besides being called padded mailers they are also called bubble mailers. They come in a variety of sizes and more importantly, they weigh next to nothing. This is important as you are going to want to ship your items in something that is not going to add much weight to the total shipment. Depending on the size of mailer, it is possible to find bubble mailers at around $0.20 - $0.30 a piece.

You can buy a standard size bubble mailer that will fit almost any book, CD, DVD, or video game. For those just starting out I would recommend buying a bubble mailer size #2 which is an 8 1/2 x 12" mailer. The bubble mailer number is universal and you should be able to find that exact size by searching for a number #2 bubble mailer on any website. While the #2 will fit most books, I find that most textbooks and larger hardcovers will not fit. For those you will need a bigger mailer such as the #4 or the #5.

As you grow your inventory and increase your sales, you will probably want different sizes of bubble mailers for specific item types. You can find mailers specifically made to fit CD's and DVD's. In the beginning, I would focus on buying only the types of mailers that can be used universally. In order to get a discount on mailers you usually have to order them by the case, and a typical case contains 100 mailers. You can also go to your local Staples or Office Depot and buy a pack of 20 or 30 bubble mailers if you are just testing the waters. If you do this, you will pay more per mailer but will not be stuck with 100 mailers if you decide that selling online is not for you.

A rigid mailer is the same shape and size of a padded mailer. The difference is that the rigid mailer is more of a corrugated box type of material. While it is a stronger material, the rigid mailer costs more per mailer and adds more weight to the shipment.

A third alternative is to ship your items in corrugated boxes. Corrugated boxes are relatively cheap and I recommend having some around in case you need them. The price for boxes depends on the size, but an average is around $0.50 per box. The box will cost a bit more than the bubble mailers and it will also add more weight to your shipment.

Keep in mind that you may have to ship some of your items in boxes. If you have a boxed set or an oversized textbook, it may not fit in a traditional mailer. Before you list an item make sure it will fit in the bubble mailer. If you need boxes be sure to buy a size that will fit the types of items you will be selling. A great size for textbooks and oversized books is the 12 x 9 x 2".

A fourth alternative is to use easy-fold mailers. Easy-fold mailers are a self seal type of box designed specifically for books and artwork. These mailers are usually too expensive to do any good and also increase your shipping costs because of their added weight. I would recommend a regular corrugated box over an easy-fold mailer as the easy-fold mailers usually run about $1.30 - $2.00 a piece.

In addition to mailers and boxes, you are going to need some labels. While you can always print your shipping labels on regular computer paper, I recommend buying some adhesive shipping labels so you do not have to spend all day taping the paper to your mailer or box. A standard shipping label size is the 8 1/2 x 5 1/2". This size comes in two labels per sheet. The label is large enough to print postage with delivery confirmation. You can find this size of label for around $0.05 - $0.10 per label.

A couple of shipping supply companies that I think are great are:
Uline - www.uline.com.
ShippingSupply.com - www.shipping supply.com.
Associated Bag Company - www.associatedbag.com.

If your business starts to pick up speed you might want to think about buying a thermal printer. These printers are made solely for printing labels and can run around $100 - $400. The great thing about thermal printers is that you are not wasting your ink or toner from your regular printer. The labels for thermal printers are also less expensive than standard shipping labels so having a thermal printer will bring your overall shipping costs down. You will also want a thermal printer if you plan to use any automated seller/shipper programs. I will be discussing those services in Chapter 7: Automation.

You should also keep some standard packing tape around and, if you are using boxes, some packaging material. You can buy plain packing paper or even use newspapers if you have them. The great thing about using bubble mailers is that they are self sealing and do not require packing paper, so you should not have to use tape. I say should not because I have had the bubble mailers not seal as securely as I would like. If this happens you can just apply a little bit of tape to each side of the seal.

Now that you know what size of mailer to use and what type of shipping label you need, you will have to get a scale in order to determine the weight of your shipment so you can print the correct postage amount. A standard postage scale is fairly inexpensive and can be found anywhere. You will probably want a 20 lb. or 30 lb. scale. I have used a 30 lb. scale ever since I started selling online. I listed some scale companies in the Appendix section and I also recommend searching on eBay or Amazon.com for scales. I recently saw a WeighMax 30 lb. scale for $19.48 on Amazon.com.

A Few More Shipping Tips

If you buy the mailers for around $0.25 and the labels for around $0.05 then you know you are spending an average of $0.30 in packaging costs per item shipped. Remember to keep that packaging cost in the back of your mind when you are bidding on items to resell or out at those garage sales. In addition, your goal should be to try to keep your total packaging cost per item sold to around $0.30 - $0.50.

Keep your packaging professional. I have seen other sellers try to cut down their shipping costs by wrapping a book they are going to sell in brown paper, taping that up, and then slapping a label on top of that. One of the problems when you continually do that, is that you will find more and more of your customers are not getting their order. The paper can easily tear, the product could fall out, and USPS is not going to re-package it for you. In fact, you will never even hear about it until the customer complains. The other downside of doing that is that it does not make you look like you are running a professional business.

Look for deals. Search eBay for bubble mailers, labels, and other supplies. I often find tons of sellers selling this stuff at incredibly low prices. I do not know how they do it and, in fact, I do not want to know.

Shipping costs matter. Remember what I said earlier about picking up your shipping supplies. If possible, it will save you big money. In fact, the more business you do, the more it will save you if you can find a shipping supply company that is close by and allows you to pick up your order.

CD and DVD cases. Either through buying bulk items at an auction or through garage and estate sales, you may come across CD's and DVD's that do not have their case. The items might still be in good condition and you are able to sell them online but it requires one additional bit of shipping supply: the case.

Even though having to buy a case for CD's and DVD's is an additional supply cost, there are cases that are inexpensive and can be used for both CD's and DVD's. The cheapest case I know of is called a "Slim Line Jewel Case". These are thinner than a traditional CD jewel case and can run around $0.17 per case. You can find these on most of the shipping supply websites listed or you can also do a search on eBay for "slim line jewel cases" and you will find plenty of sellers supplying that product.

CHAPTER 5:
CUSTOMER SERVICE

One of the keys to selling online is to maintain a high feedback rating. All of the sites that you will be selling on allow the buyer to leave feedback about the seller. It is in your best interest as a seller to protect and grow positive feedback. After all, with the number of different sellers out there, the main thing that can set you apart is your feedback score. There are a number of factors that will influence a buyer's decision to leave feedback. These include the shipping speed, the item description, and how returns/refunds are handled.

Shipping

The speed at which the customer receives their order is one of the main factors that influence your feedback. I find that I get more feedback stating, "fast shipping" or "prompt delivery" than anything else. When you are selling used books you are most likely going to be stuck shipping items via Media Mail which has a delivery time of around 2 - 9 days. This is an estimate as Media Mail can take up to a couple of weeks or more, especially when shipped to Alaska or Hawaii.

To minimize any complaints about delivery times it is best to ship your item either the day you receive the order or the next day. This will ensure that your package will reach your customer as fast as possible. In addition, you should send an e-mail to the buyer with tracking information.

Most of the sites you will be selling on have a generic "contact the buyer" link where you can submit tracking information while some sites will give you the buyer's e-mail address. If you have the buyer's e-mail address you can enter it when you are processing the order for shipment with an online postage company like Endicia. Once you buy the postage an automatic e-mail will be sent to the e-mail address you entered, giving the buyer a shipment confirmation as well as tracking information.

Submitting tracking information to the buyer is going to decrease the amount of e-mails you may get with people looking for their package. This way, your buyers can simply look up the information on their own which will save you valuable time. In addition, buyers will appreciate you letting them know that their item was shipped out as quickly as possible.

An e-mail to your customer with tracking information should look something like this:

Dear Customer,

Thank you for your recent order. It was shipped (date) via the U.S. Postal Service. You can track your package at http://www.usps.com using tracking #(insert tracking number).

Thank you for your business,
(Your seller name)

Item Description

Besides shipping, the other main factor that is going to affect your feedback rating is your item description. Did you give the buyer an honest appraisal of the item? If you sold a book listed as "like new" but it is highlighted and has a torn cover then you are probably going to get some negative feedback. If selling CD's and DVD's did you mention any large scratches on the disc? Or that the video game does not include the original game manual?

If you follow the condition guidelines outlined in this book and found on the sites you will be selling on, then you should not run into many problems with bad feedback being associated with your item description. Buyers will appreciate your honesty and are more likely to leave positive feedback if you give them the item they ordered in the condition they expect, if not better. Just remember to describe your item's benefits as well as the negatives.

Returns

How you handle your customer's complaints and concerns will also have an impact on the type of feedback a customer will leave. Even if the customer returns an item or states that the item was never received, they can still leave you feedback about the transaction.

The first thing you want to do concerning customer service is to agree upon a return policy. Sometimes the return policy is going to be dictated by whatever site you end up selling on. For the most part, expect to have a 30 day return policy for new and used items. Returns for new items should only be made if the item is unopened or if the shipment was compromised because of your mistake.

The 30 day return policy is a general policy that most sellers incorporate, but you are free to offer a more generous policy if you choose to. If you describe your items honestly and focus on fast shipping then you should have a refund rate of less than 1%.

If a customer wants to return an item, one of the best things you can do for your feedback rating is to send them a pre-paid mailer for them to send back the item. You can instruct them to put the item in the mailer and drop it off at the U.S. Post Office. This will be done at a loss for you but think of it as the cost of doing business. In the end, a great feedback score is going to drive more sales and make up for your loss of $2.50 on a few returns here and there. And this is another important reason why it pays to be honest in your descriptions as customers are less likely to return items that are of the quality they expected.

There are some cases where the cost of shipping the customer a pre-paid mailer is more than what you would get if you resold the item. In this case you can simply instruct the customer to keep the item, issue them a refund, and write off the cost. For example, if it costs $2.50 to send them a pre-paid mailer then you are out $2.50 plus your first shipping cost of $2.50 for a total of $5.00. If you can only make $3.00 off of that item then you might as well just let the customer keep it. Perhaps they are requesting a refund because of the quality. If this is the case, and you are fine with them keeping the product, you can send an e-mail similar to this one to try to cultivate some good feedback from a buyer who may not be pleased:

Dear Customer,

I understand that there is a problem with the quality the item you received from us. I apologize for any issue regarding the condition of your item. Our policy has always been to accurately describe the condition of the items we list. If you are not happy with the item then neither are we. A full refund will be issued to you. In addition, you are free to keep the item that was shipped to you as we do not currently have the same item in a better condition.

Thank you for your business,

(Your seller name)

You might also get complaints from customers who received the exact item they requested in the exact condition as described. My return policy is to accept returns within 30 days but I will not pay for shipping back to me if the correct item was shipped and the item was in the exact condition as described.

The e-mails are not always courteous but do not take this personally, just keep it professional and try to resolve the situation as quickly as possible. One recent example was that I sold a HD-DVD movie. I had a new and sealed copy of the movie. The buyer thought that this was a regular DVD although it was correctly listed as the HD-DVD format. In response, the buyer sent me an e-mail that was similar to this:

HEY, EVERYTHING WAS GOOD EXCEPT THIS DOES NOT WORK IN MY DVD PLAYER. IN OTHER WORDS YOU WERE A COMPLETE WASTE OF TIME AND YOU STOLE MY MONEY.

So, shipping the correct item ordered and in the exact condition as described made me a thief to this customer. Well, when I read his e-mail it seemed to me that the person did not know what a HD-DVD was. Perhaps people have already forgotten since Blu-ray won the high definition DVD battle not too long ago; but HD-DVD's can only be played in a HD-DVD player just like a Blu-ray DVD can only run on a Blu-ray player.

In response to this customer's e-mail I sent him something similar to this:

Dear Customer,

I understand there was a problem with your recent order. I looked into the issue and confirmed that the item ordered was the correct item shipped. This item is a HD-DVD movie and will only work in a HD-DVD player.

If you were trying to buy this movie in the standard DVD format then I can give you a partial refund of 65% of the item price since this was a new item that has been opened.

You can send returns to:

[My Address]
Sincerely yours,
[My Seller Name]

Since this was a new item that was opened and because it was the correct item shipped, I did not have to offer him a refund at all. However, many times just the offer of a refund is enough to persuade the customer not to leave bad feedback. Although, there may be times when you receive bad feedback even if you did everything right.

In fact, I have received bad feedback in the past simply because the customer did not like the movie they ordered; I guess they thought they were leaving a review of the item itself and not of the seller. I will show you how you can try to get negative feedback removed in a bit.

Refunds

In addition to a few customers requesting a return, you are bound to have a few problem deliveries where the buyer is requesting a refund because the product was never received. If you send your items with tracking information you will be able to see if the item was received and when it was delivered. There are a number of reasons why a customer would not have received your item:

- The item could have been stolen after delivery.
- The Post Office could have delivered the item to the wrong address.
- The packaging for the item could have been damaged and rendered the address unreadable.
- The package could have come open during shipment and the item has fallen out.
- The package is still in transit.

In most cases it is best to take your buyer's word for it and issue a refund after an appropriate amount of time has passed. In addition, instruct your customer to ask their neighbor if they received the package or their postal carrier who scanned the package as delivered, if possible. In the end, you may just be forced to refund the item.

If you are sending a high priced item you might want to consider buying shipping insurance. It typically only costs a couple of dollars and if you are going to make $20 - $50 on that order then why not insure that income. This way you will avoid the negative feedback you will get if you just tell the buyer your tracking information states the package was delivered.

Asking For Feedback

Another way to get feedback from your customers is to solicit it after your item has been delivered. After you sell an item on most of the seller sites, including Amazon.com, the operator of the site will send an e-mail to the customer asking them to leave you feedback. Amazon.com sends an e-mail 30 days after the order with instructions on how to leave you feedback.

I find that around 10% of customers will leave feedback without any soliciting. Soliciting right after your item was delivered with your own e-mail can increase this amount to around 20%. To do this, simply go into your online postage account and search for delivered items. You can then send e-mails to those buyers requesting feedback. A sample feedback solicitation e-mail looks like this:

Dear Customer,

Thank you for your recent order. Our goal is to provide you with excellent service. If you are satisfied with our service please leave us feedback on [seller site]. If unsatisfied for any reason please contact us before leaving feedback and we will be happy to resolve the situation.

You can leave feedback for me by logging onto your account at [seller site], review your recent orders, and click on the "leave seller feedback" link.

Thank you for your business,

[Your seller name]

A typical feedback solicitation e-mail should thank the customer for their order, ask for feedback, let the customer know of a way to resolve problems before giving negative feedback, and include instructions on how to leave feedback.

Removing Negative Feedback

Even if you do everything right, you will inevitably receive some negative feedback. However, there are ways to try to get this feedback removed. If the negative feedback is simply a review of the product and not of you as a seller, you can contact the seller site you are selling on and ask them to remove that feedback since it is not a seller feedback but a product review.

In addition, you can find out who the buyer is and then send them an e-mail asking them to remove the feedback. Anyone who leaves feedback can go back to their account and easily delete it. Below is a sample e-mail that you can send to a customer who has left a negative review of the product to your seller account.

Dear Customer,

I recently noticed feedback related to your purchase of [Item Purchased] on [date purchased] posted to my seller ac-

count. *Please note that the feedback left is a review of the product and not a review of my service as a seller.*

Negative feedback has a large impact on my sales. If you feel I provided you with excellent service (shipped the item on time, shipped the correct item, and item was delivered in the condition promised) please delete or edit your negative feedback by logging into your account, view the order referenced above, and select the feedback left.

From there you can leave me seller feedback based on my service. If you wish to leave a review of the product you purchased please go to the product's detail page on [site sold on] and click on the "review product link".

Thank you for your business,
[Your seller name]

You can use the same general e-mail format to ask for the removal of bad feedback in any circumstance. Perhaps the customer left you bad feedback because they felt the product took too long to get there. If you shipped the order the same day or the next day you can stress that to them and let them know that you did everything you could to get the package delivered in a timely manner. You could also offer to refund the shipping cost for the removal of bad feedback.

This will often work, however, there are plenty of customers who just might not care. Try your best to get the feedback removed but, more importantly, focus on shipping out your products and providing a great service. Doing so will cultivate more good feedback than bad.

CHAPTER 6:
INVENTORY MANAGEMENT

Effectively managing your inventory is going to save you both time and money. You need to be active in organizing your inventory from the start. This will help you to find products that have been ordered as well as enable you to make the most out of the space you are using. You also need to monitor how long you have had an item in your inventory and what to do about stock that has grown stale.

The SKU System

Most sellers will organize their inventory by alphabetical order when they first start selling. This is fine for sellers with small inventories that they can easily keep track of. Once you are maintaining inventories of 500+ items, you will find some major problems with the alphabet system.

One problem is that you may have the same book, CD, DVD, or video game but in different conditions. You might forget this and grab the first one you see which could be a condition worse than the one that was ordered. Also, you will find that you are constantly trying to reorganize the items on the shelves to fit in alphabetical order.

A better inventory management solution is to use a SKU system. SKU stands for stock keeping unit; and instead of basing where you store your inventory on the alphabet, you will do it based on a location and a number. This ensures that each item has a unique number that cannot be confused with any other item.

An example of a SKU system for a seller shipping books, CD's, DVD's, and video games is to have a unique location and number for each item. If you have four shelves you can select one shelf for each type of item. If you do this your first SKU's would be B1, DVD1, CD1, and VG1. When you are listing your inventory you just need to keep adding the SKU number based on the product and the last SKU you had. So, your first four books would be B1, B2, B3, B4 and you would stock them in that order on your B shelf. You would do the same for your DVD, CD, and VG shelves.

Once you assign a SKU to your item, you will need to label your item. This can be done by using removable labels that do not leave any residue. Avery makes removable labels of all different sizes. I would recommend the 6460 or 6466. These labels can be found at your local Staples or Office Depot or just go to www.Avery.com and you can order direct from the manufacturer.

Cleaning Out Your Closet

In addition to a SKU system, you need a way to easily see how long you have had some items in your inventory. If these are low priced items then you need to think about having some way of removing them in order to make room for new inventory. If you have the SKU number you can always look up your inventory in your database, or the site you are selling on, and see when you listed that item.

Another alternative is to use a colored removable inventory label. You can structure each color to represent a month of the year. If you maintain an inventory of 500 + items I recommend that you save a day each month and go through items that have been in your inventory for at least three full months. You may want to shorten or lengthen that time span depending on your own inventory policies. You can find removable color inventory labels from most shipping supply and label companies, such as Uline.

An example of using the color-coded technique is if you are starting to sell in January you label the items listed in January with red removable labels. You will label February yellow, March green, and so on. Set aside a day in the beginning of May to go through all your reds. Doing so will give all that initial inventory three full months to sell (February, March, April. Do not include January as you might have listed the item in the middle or end of the month). Just be sure to keep a reference guide as to what month coincides with what inventory color.

What do you do with your stale inventory? You have a number of options. If the item is still selling for a good price you can keep it in your inventory. I would say anything with a list price of $5.00 or more can be kept. If the item is currently selling for anything less than $5.00 I would recommend a few things.

One way to clean your closet is to bulk list your stale inventory on eBay. If you do this be sure to list each title in the auction as this will help encourage bids. I also find that selling all like items in one auction works the best. For example, if I have multiple horror DVD's I will list them in a pack of five or ten horror films. If I have a bunch of mystery books I will list those together as a mystery book collection auction. The most important thing is to take a clean picture of your items and list the titles of each item.

You can also give them away to a library or a thrift store. However, since you are also buying from libraries and thrift stores you will have to remember that you can run across your old dead inventory from time to time. Despite this risk, aside from simply throwing the items in the trash, it is sometimes the only way to get rid of your stale stock and free up inventory space.

A third option is to trade the books with a used bookstore. This way you will have credit at the bookstore and then you can hunt for more deals without having to pay that much more, if anything.

Is Storage an Issue?

One of the things I like about focusing on selling used books, CD's, DVD's, and video games is that they are relatively small items and do not take up too much space. Of course, as your inventory grows you may be constantly looking for places to store your inventory. If possible, I recommend a dedicated room in your residence. On top of that you may also need to utilize as much garage or basement space as possible.

As you grow your business you may find that you are completely out of space. If you decide to take it to the next level and rent a storage space, make sure you are bringing in the type of income that is going to make it worth your while to rent a space out.

One quick and cheap fix to running out of space is to rent a storage unit. The units are drastically cheaper than renting an office space and can provide plenty of room. One of the biggest storage rental companies is Public Storage: www.publicstorage.com.

The only problem with using a storage facility is the inconvenience of having to go there almost every day to pick up the products that you are shipping out and to drop off your new inventory.

Price Adjusting

Sellers are constantly outbidding each other to have the lowest price available. It is a good idea to weekly or bi-weekly re-adjust your prices to either the lowest or as close to the lowest price as possible. This ensures that your item will always be seen by as many buyers as possible. No one is going to want to spend more money to buy the same product from you if they can get it from someone else for less money, unless there is something unique about the item you are selling.

CHAPTER 7:
AUTOMATION

Think about how great it would be if you could scan all of the items that you wanted to sell into one database and upload the database into a program which would then, not only list those items on any number of websites, but would also automatically price your items based on your pricing parameters. Better yet, when those items sell, think about how easy it would be to print packing slips and labels from one database which is linked to your online postage provider. In addition, once the order shipped an automated e-mail would be sent to your buyer letting them know that you are providing them with excellent service.

This is not just a dream; it is the 21st century and technology is here to help. There are a number of software programs that will allow you to save time by automating all aspects of your online business. This will enable you to spend more time managing your inventory and searching for new items to sell online.

The time saved using these services can be incredible. If you have a service that allows you to scan in your items and automatically price them, it can save you a week of work. For example, if you list 500 items a week you are going to have to look up each item, go to that item's detail page to see the prices of your competitors, decide on a price, and create a listing for the item. It is no joke that this can take around five minutes an item, and that is just when selling on one channel, such as

Amazon.com. With 500 items that would come out to 2,500 minutes of listing, which equates to over 41 hours of work. One entire work week of eight hours a day just to list your items, and you have not even sold anything yet! With an automated solution you can list your items within a few hours and then focus on other aspects of your business.

There are different types of automated software packages out there. Some are complete solutions which are applications that allow you to input inventory into one database, list inventory on multiple sales channels, manage pricing, confirm orders, and ship orders all from one central program. The software is connected to the various websites you will be selling on so there is no need to go back and forth through the different sites. The software will list the items on the available channels and, when sold, it will pull the items off the other channels so you do not have to worry about selling an item you have just sold on a different site.

Other applications are simply listing tools or types of automated re-pricing software. The software companies usually charge a monthly service fee to use their programs, and some charge a fee based on the number of items you have or a percentage of your sales. Because of the number of companies out there who provide the same type of service, I think the fees are actually quite reasonable considering the amount of time you will be able to save.

The move to an automated program should be made as you get more serious with your business. If you are just going to be cleaning out your garage, then you probably do not have to worry about it. However, if you are continually bringing in around 200 or so items per week then you are going to want to consider ways to run your business more efficiently. Included in this chapter is a list of vendors who provide automation software:

Automation Software

AMan Pro - www.spaceware.com

AMan Pro is a recommend solution for sellers on Amazon.com. This software will help you to list your items in bulk, automate pricing based on your criteria, manage your orders, and works with Endicia to print postage.

They currently offer a free 21 day trial. After the trial, the service is $49.99 per month or you can pay an annual fee of $499.

FillZ - www.fillz.com

FillZ is a complete seller solution and one that I highly recommend. FillZ will allow you to list your products on up to 20 fixed-price sales channels. Auction sales channels such as eBay are not currently supported. You can only list on eBay through FillZ if you have an eBay Store.

The company offers two different packages: Standard and Premium. The Standard is recommended for low to medium sales volumes. The Standard service will cost you the greater of $50.00 a month for revenue under $3,000 or $1.00 per every 1,000th item listed. If you have over $3,000 of revenue a month then the fee is calculated by a percentage of that revenue.

The Standard package will enable you to sell across 20 channels, manage your inventory, manage your orders, customize pricing, send confirmation e-mails, and print postage through Endicia.

ChannelMax - www.channelmax.net

ChannelMax is another complete software solution. They currently offer support for sellers on Amazon.com, Half.com, eBay, and Abebooks. The company sells software that will allow you to upload and list your items on the supported channels, manage inventory, automate re-pricing on Amazon.com, send confirmation e-mails, and print postage through DHL, Endicia, UPS, FedEx, and Stamps.com.

BookRouter - www.bookrouter.com

BookRouter was specifically designed for books. The software is not a complete seller solution but it makes it easy for you to list your items on multiple sales channels at the same time. Once you have your inventory in a database you can upload that database to BookRouter, set your pricing, and it will be listed on the websites you choose. As of 2009, there were around 18 different websites you could choose from.

There is a $50.00 initial set-up fee. The set-up fee allows you to choose five different sales channels and it is $5.00 for each additional site. After the initial set-up fee you will be charged $25.00 per month for up to five sites and $5.00 for each additional site.

ChannelAdvisor - www.channeladvisor.com

Channel Advisor offers a complete seller solution for the professional seller. Their pricing and programs are based on your sales volume and your specific needs. You can go to their website and contact them for pricing that is tailored to your individual needs.

RepriceIt - www.repriceit.com

Repriceit offers a solution to pricing your inventory on Amazon.com. You can set certain pricing criteria and the program will automatically price your inventory. The company offers a 30 day free trial. After the free trial, the fee is $9.95 per month.

Mail Extractor - www.mailextractor.com

Mail Extractor provides an automated shipping solution to sellers on Amazon.com, Half.com, eBay, and Alibris. The program will import orders from the websites, create packing slips, print postage through Endicia, and send automated shipment e-mails to customers. The fee for this service starts at only $7.95.

Seller Engine - www.sellerengine.com

Seller engine offers a listing and inventory management solution for sellers on Amazon.com. The program will allow you to quickly list items on Amazon.com, manage your inventory, and e-mail customers. The software also provides automated re-pricing. The company offers a free trial of one month. After the free trial, the fee is $49.95 per month.

Seller Magic - www.sellermagic.com

Seller Magic offers a listing and inventory management solution to sellers on Amazon.com. The software program will allow you to upload your inventory, set pricing criteria, and automatically re-price your listings. The company offers seven days of free service. You can also try the software with up to 10 products to see how you like it before any purchase. The subscription rate for the software is $29.95 per month.

HomeBase - www.abebooks.com/books/homebase/main-.shtml

HomeBase is a free inventory management program distributed by Abebooks.com. The program is designed specifically for books.

eBay.com – http://pages.ebay.com/help/sell/advanced_selling_tools.html

eBay offers a number of listing and inventory management solutions to sellers on their website. If you are going to sell specifically on eBay then I advise you to check out the services that eBay provides.

Turbo Lister - Turbo Lister is a free program distributed by eBay. The program will let you upload multiple listings at once.

Selling Manager - Selling Manager costs $4.99 per month and will help you manage all of your listings.

Selling Manager Pro - Selling Manager Pro costs $15.99 per month and includes some inventory management and automation tools.

Blackthorne Basic - Blackthorne Basic costs $9.99 per month. The program is a desktop application that lets you create and manage listings as well as provides some automation when dealing with buyer communication.

Blackthorne Pro - Blackthorne Pro costs $24.99 per month. The program is also a desktop application that includes all features of the Blackthorne Basic plus some inventory management and reporting features.

Scanners

I mentioned scanners in Chapter 2 when I was discussing how to price items while you were out in the field. The other reason to invest in a scanner is so you can fully automate your listing process. Once you have a scanner, you simply scan the barcode and, depending on your automation software, the information will be captured in your database file. You then upload this database file and the software will create listings for you. This will save you the time of typing in every ISBN number and book title.

As noted before, scanners can be quite expensive. If you are a professional seller then I think investing in a scanner would make sense. Your best bet is to look on eBay and Amazon.com first to see if you can find any used scanners. Aside from that, you can look into the shipping supply companies listed in Appendix 3. Most of the shipping supply companies carry an assortment of different scanners. Also included in Appendix 3 are companies that specialize in scanners; these include stand alone scanners and scanners for an internet enabled phone.

CHAPTER 8:
SETTING UP YOUR BUSINESS

Before you rush headfirst into actively purchasing items to sell online, you will want to take care of the legal aspects of operating a business. I will give you a basic outline of what to expect as a seller and the basic outlines of the different business types that you can set up, but I recommend that as your business grows you consider hiring a Certified Public Accountant (CPA) to advise you on your specific tax situation.

Different states have different requirements and your local CPA will be able to give you the best advice on how to set up the most efficient business structure. CPA's can be hired to handle your entire bookkeeping process; this will free up the time you will need to be actively buying and selling your products. After all, you are going to be a seller, not an accountant.

That being said, you can get by doing some basic accounting yourself and, as you gain experience and start making more money, you can think about looking for a good CPA. I would still advise that you go to a CPA to report your state and federal income taxes for at least your first year. Your CPA will be able to guide you through the process and make reporting your taxes as headache free as possible.

Most states have a Society of CPA's. You can find this by doing a Google search for: [Your state] society of CPA's. You can also find local CPA's by simply using your phone book or going to www.yellowpages.com. You will want a CPA that has been in business for a number of years and who can provide you with bookkeeping, tax, and consultation services. There are many good CPA's out there and you should have no problem finding one in your general area.

Types of Businesses

If you are just selling your used items then most states will consider that as more of a hobby or garage sale type of activity. You are not actively buying items for resale but are selling your prior purchases. That being said, if you sell those items for more than you paid for them then you are required to pay tax on the difference that you made. So, even at this level of selling you are going to want to keep detailed records, and I will show you what to focus on in a bit.

The first thing you need to do when you are starting your business is to apply for a business license. A business license is obtained in the city you are going to be operating out of. Most cities have their own website and you can do an internet search of your city to find it; there you will find the information of how to obtain a business license from your city. The license is usually inexpensive and can run around $50.00 depending on the city and what type of sales revenue you are going to have. When you apply for your business license you will need to describe the legal structure of your business. The main types of businesses are: sole proprietorship, partnership, limited liability company, and corporation.

Sole Proprietorship

A sole proprietorship is the most basic type of business. It is a business entity that has no separation from the owner. This means that any liability from operating the business is the owner's liability. In other words, if the company is sued, the owner is held personally liable.

The benefits are that a sole proprietorship is simple to set up. You simply apply for your business license as a sole proprietorship. In addition, the income tax feature is relatively simple; you do not pay corporate taxes but rather pay self employment taxes on the profits made in addition to your regular income tax. This simplifies the accounting process.

Partnership

A partnership is similar to that of sole proprietorship except that in this case there are at least two parties involved. The parties will share the profits, losses, and liabilities of the company. The rules that govern partnerships are dependent on the jurisdiction in which it operates.

Limited Liability Company

A limited liability company is also known as an LLC. This type of company is traditionally the next step from a sole proprietorship. It includes many of the benefits of a sole proprietorship as well as the limited liability of a corporation.

A LLC has the flexibility of choosing how to report taxes. The LLC can be taxed as a sole proprietor, partnership, S-Corporation, or C-Corporation. Of course, the jurisdiction of the LLC also comes into play as some states levy a franchise tax or capital values tax on LLC's.

Corporation

A corporation is probably the type of business we are most familiar with. Large businesses are usually corporations; they are separate and individual legal entities. The limited liability of a corporation makes it an attractive business type for those doing a large amount of sales.

One aspect of a corporation that concerns taxes is the issue of "double taxation". The profit of a corporation is taxed at a corporate tax rate. Any income that is distributed to employees, owners, or shareholders is then taxed at that individual's income tax rate; hence, the issue of "double taxation".

Business License and Sales Tax

DBA

Once you decide on a business type and complete the necessary registrations for businesses other than a sole proprietorship, you can complete your request for a business license from the city you are going to be operating out of.

If you decide to set up as a sole proprietorship you may also want to file for a DBA. DBA stands for "Doing Business As" and it allows you to pick a name for your business instead of using your legal name. This is a simple process and all you need to do is to visit your local county clerk's office.

Sales Tax Permit

If you are buying tangible items for the purpose of resale then you are going to have to obtain a sales permit from your state. The instructions for how to do this should be found on your state's board of equalization, or tax board, website. The permits are usually free of charge and filing the permits will register your business to remit sales tax to your state's tax board.

As of August 2009, you are required to pay sales tax on all sales within your state. This means that you do not have to remit sales tax based on internet sales made outside of the state you are operating out of.

One benefit of having a sales permit is that it allows you to obtain a resale certificate from vendors. You will be able to purchase items you are going to resell without having to pay the tax on the purchase. Of course, you have to remit the tax on the sale of the item if it is shipped within the state you operate out of.

Further Business and Tax Resources

Your local city will have plenty of resources available to you on how to best set up your business structure; I advise you to find your city's website and go through their free information. You will also want to gather as much information from your state's tax board or board of equalization. I also mention a number of books specifically on how to best set up your business from a tax and legal standpoint in the recommended reading section.

In addition, you can go to www.irs.gov. This is the main website for the Internal Revenue Service. In particular, I recommend checking out the following IRS publications which are free to download on www.irs.gov:

1. Publication 334 - Tax Guide for Small Business
2. Publication 535 - Business Expenses
3. Publication 583 – Starting a Business and Keeping Records
4. Publication 587 - Business Use of Your Home

Basic Accounting

Your accounting practices can be basic at first. The main thing is to keep an accurate and up to date record of all your income and expenses. There are two main types of accounting: cash accounting and accrual accounting. Cash accounting is a type of accounting where the income and expenses are recorded in the period in which the money is received or paid. Accrual accounting is described as, "an accounting method that measures the performance and position of a company by recognizing economic events regardless of when cash transactions occur".(19)

According to the IRS, only certain businesses can use the cash accounting method, "Generally, if you produce, purchase, or sell merchandise in your business, you must keep an inventory and use the accrual method for purchases and sales of merchandise".(20) Since you would be purchasing and selling merchandise you would actually have to use the accrual method of accounting. The IRS does list a few exceptions to this rule. One of them is that if your annual gross sales are under $1 million then you can use the cash accounting method. The full article where this information is located can be found on the IRS website and looking up the publication recommended earlier: Publication 334 - Tax Guide for Small Business.

Now that you know you can use the cash accounting method, how do you? Well, this is a simple and easy accounting method to use. You are going to be writing off expenses as you pay for them and income as it comes in. In reality, a true cash accounting system does not account for standing inventory but rather expenses inventory as it is paid for.

For example, say you are starting a business with $100.00. When you set up your accounting software you should see $100.00 in cash in your bank account on your balance sheet. You then pay $50.00 for a business license which can be expensed to a "license and tax account". Now, you will see $50.00 of expense on your income statement and a net income of -$50.00. You then buy $25.00 of books at a garage sale. This transaction is expensed under Cost of Goods Sold/Inventory. You will now see an expense of $50.00 for the license and $25.00 under COGS for the inventory for a total expense of $75.00; your net income would show -$75.00.

You then begin to sell the books and make $125.00 in the same month. The $125.00 will be entered under the income account as "sales". Your income statement will now show a total net profit of $50.00 since you booked sales of $125.00 and expensed $75.00. The bank account on your balance sheet should show $150.00 since you started with $100.00, subtracted $75.00 in paid expenses, and added $125.00 in received money for sales. For a further and more detailed explanation of accounting and how to keep your records, I included some small business and accounting books in the recommended reading section of this book.

The main problem with cash accounting is that it is hard to evaluate how your business is performing month to month. For example, if you pay for a bunch of supplies in March you will write all of them off as expenses in March. April may then show a lot less expense and therefore seem to be more profitable. In reality, you have expensed the supplies you are actually using in April in March.

There are plenty of accounting software programs out there and some of them are even free. Go to http://quickbooks.intuit.com and check out the QuickBooks Simple Start Free Edition. This is a free and simple accounting software program that will allow you to track your income and expenses.

Besides QuickBooks, the other type of accounting software that is popular is called Quicken. Either QuickBooks or Quicken will work just fine. You should also maintain a paper trail of your transactions in case you are ever audited. The recommended time-frame for keeping documentation is typically around seven years.

As I recommended before, if your business is picking up steam fast you might want to look into hiring a CPA to handle your entire bookkeeping process. If you are able to do this, your time will be free to focus on growing your business instead of worrying about how to pay your taxes. Your local CPA will also be an expert in your state's tax procedures as they relate to your business's legal structure.

APPENDIX 1:
SELLER WEBSITE LIST

In addition to selling your products on the websites I have discussed in detail, you can also sell your products on the websites listed in this Appendix.

A1Books - www.a1books.com

Abebooks - www.abebooks.com

Alibris.com - www.alibris.com

Amazon.com - www.amazon.com

Barnes & Noble - www.barnesandnoble.com

Biblio.com - www.biblio.com

Books-a-Million - www.booksamillion.com

Borders - www.borders.com

Buy.com - www.buy.com

Cash 4 Books – www.cash4books.net

Cash For CD's – www.cashforcds.com

CheapBooks – www.cheapbooks.com

Chrislands.com - www.chrislands.com

Choosebooks.com - www.choosebooks.com

Craigslist - www.craigslist.org

DVD Pawn – www.dvdpawn.com

eBay.com - www.ebay.com

ecampus.com - www.ecampus.com

gemm - www.gemm.com

Half.com - www.half.com

Overstock - www.overstock.com

SecondSpin.com – www.secondspin.com

Sell.com Classifieds - www.sell.com

Sell My DVD's – www.sellmydvds.com

TextbooksRus - www.textbooksrus.com

Textbookx - www.textbookx.com

Valore Books - www.valorebooks.com

APPENDIX 2:
BUYING ITEMS FOR RESALE
WEBSITE LIST

In addition to the physical auctions, estate sales, and garage sales that you can attend, you can use the Internet to find a variety of items to sell online. This Appendix includes places to find used stuff to sell as well as where to find new books, CD's, DVD's, and video games online.

Used Items

PropertyRoom.com - www.propertyroom.com

U.S. Treasury Department Online Auctions - www.govsales.gov

eBay.com - www.ebay.com

Craigslist - www.craigslist.org

Remainder Book Wholesalers

A1 Overstock - www.a1overstock.com

American Book Company - www.americanbookco.com

Bargain Books Wholesale - www.bargainbookswholesale.com

The Book Depot - www.bookdepot.com

Book Sales, Inc. - www.booksalesusa.com

Daedalus Books Wholesale - www.daedalus-wholesale.com

Love for Books - www.loveforbooks.com

New Products

Ingram Entertainment, Inc. - www.ingramentertainment.com
Ingram is one of the largest distributors for DVD's, video games, and audio books.

Ingram Book Company - www.ingrambook.com

Baker & Taylor - www.btol.com
Baker & Taylor focuses on books, movies, and music.

Mountain View Movies - www.mountainviewmovies.com

APPENDIX 3:
ONLINE POSTAGE
AND
SHIPPING SUPPLIERS

Online Postage Companies
(listed by recommended companies first):

Endicia - www.endicia.com

Stamps.com - www.stamps.com

PayPal - www.paypal.com
Note: Postage here can only be printed for items sold on eBay, Half.com, or directly through PayPal.

U.S. Post Office Click-N-Ship - www.usps.com

PitneyBowes - www.pb.com

Shipping Supply Companies
(listed by recommended companies first):

Amazon.com - www.amazon.com
Search on Amazon.com for any type of shipping supply such as bubble mailers, boxes, labels, and even tape.

eBay.com - www.ebay.com
You can also find great deals on shipping supplies by searching on eBay.

Uline - www.uline.com

Associated Bag Company - www.associatedbag.com

ShippingSupply.com - www.shippingsupply.com

PackagingPrice.com - www.packagingprice.com

Paper Mart - www.papermart.com

AM Shipping Supplies Company, Inc.
- www.amshippingsupplies.com

PackagingSupplies.com - www.packagingsupplies.com

JustShippingSupplies.com - www.justshippingsupplies.com

Compass Packaging - www.shippingsupplies.net

Staples - www.staples.com

Office Depot - www.officedepot.com

EZ Shipping Supply - www.ezshippingsupply.com

Quill - www.quill.com

Boxes Cheaper - www.boxescheaper.com

Northern Safety & Industrial - www.northernsafety.com

Fast-Pack.com - www.fast-pack.com

OurShippingSupplies.com - www.ourshippingsupplies.com

esupplystore.com - www.esupplystore.com

Packit Right - www.packitright.net

Monster Packaging - www.monsterpackaging.com

The Box Company, Inc. - http://boxco.shoppkg.com

OfficeMax - www.officemax.com

Shipping Scales

(listed by recommended companies first):

Amazon.com - www.amazon.com
Do a search for shipping scales and you will find plenty of affordable scales on Amazon.com.

eBay.com - www.ebay.com
As with Amazon.com, there are plenty of sellers selling affordable scales on eBay.

SaveOnScales.com - www.saveonscales.com

ScalesOnline.com - www.scalesonline.com

Scales Galore - www.scalesgalore.com

All-Scale - www.allscale.com

Scanners

(listed by recommended companies first):

Scout Pal - www.scoutpal.com

Media Scouter - www.mediascouter.com

A Seller Tool - www.asellertool.com

APPENDIX 4:
EXAMPLES OF MY SALES

I wanted to include some examples of products I have sold so that you can get a better idea of the types of products to be on the lookout for. I purchased the following items through a combination of garage sales, estate sales, thrift stores, used bookstores, and various auctions.

These have been some of my biggest sales based on profit margin. Of course, the prices of these items can change over time so I would advise you to double check the item price online if you should come across them. Also, do not expect to make a 1,000% profit on each item you sell. When you buy in bulk at auctions, you will inevitably find a number of gems along the way. I would say that once you gain some experience, and if you are conservative in your purchases, you should be able to have an average selling price of around $5.00 - $10.00. If you spend an average of $2.00 or less per item then you should be fine; of course, the less you spend, the more you are going to make.

Books

Textbooks can lead to huge gains when you find a recent textbook and can get it at a decent price. I have found a lot of textbooks at police auctions. The textbooks I find at garage sales tend to be of an older variety and can be hard to resell. It is important with a textbook to find out if it is the most recent edition or if it is still in demand before you spend too much money purchasing it to sell online. Aside from textbooks, my biggest profits have come from finding great deals on nonfiction books, particularly in the investing and philosophy areas.

Textbook: *Guide to Clinical Trials by Spilker, Bert.*
Profit after commissions = $129.75.
My purchase cost = $2.50.
Gross profit margin = 5,090%.

Textbook: *Semiconductor Wafer Bonding: Science and Technology by Tong, Q.*
Profit after commissions = $78.75.
My purchase cost = $2.50.
Gross profit margin = 3,050%.

Textbook: *Numerical and Analytical Methods for Scientists and Engineers, Using Mathmatica by Dubin, D.*
Profit after commissions = $66.04.
My purchase cost = $1.75.
Gross profit margin = 3,673%.

Nonfiction/Investing: *Come Into My Trading Room: A Complete Guide to Trading by Elder, A.*
Profit after commissions = $27.75.
My purchase cost = $1.75.
Gross profit margin = 1,485%.

Nonfiction/Investing: *Trend Following: How Great Traders Make Millions in Up or Down Markets by Covel, M.*
Profit after commissions = $17.52.
My purchase cost = $3.00.
Gross profit margin = 484%.

Nonfiction/Investing: *Asset Allocation: Balancing Financial Risk by Gibson, R.*
Profit after commissions = $17.13.
My purchase cost = $2.50.
Gross profit margin = 585%.

Nonfiction/Investing: *Trading for Dummies by Griffis, M.*
Profit after commissions = $15.00.
My purchase cost = $1.50.
Gross profit margin = 900%.

Nonfiction/Photographs: *John Szarkowski: Photographs by Szarkowski, J. and Phillips, S.*
Profit after commissions = $23.08.
My purchase cost = $2.00.
Gross profit margin = 1,054%.

Nonfiction: *The Beatles Anthology [Hardcover] by Beatles, Lennon, J., McCartney, P., and Harrison, G.*
Profit after commissions = $18.79.
My purchase cost = $1.50.
Gross profit margin = 1,152%.

Nonfiction: *All Clear!: Idioms in Context by Fragiadakis, H.*
Profit after commissions = $17.76.
My purchase cost = $2.00.
Gross profit margin = 788%.

Nonfiction/Philosophy: *Free Will by Kane, R.*
Profit after commissions = $17.37.
My purchase cost = $1.75.
Gross profit margin = 892%.

Nonfiction: *Origins of Zionism by Vital, D.*
Profit after commissions = $10.75.
My purchase cost = $1.00.
Gross profit margin = 975%.

Nonfiction: *Beginning Shepherd's Manual by Smith, B.*
Profit after commissions = $24.10.
My purchase cost = $2.00.
Gross profit margin = 1,105%.

Nonfiction: *Images of Organization by Morgan, G.*
Profit after commissions = $21.38.
My purchase cost = $1.75.
Gross profit margin = 1,121%.

Nonfiction/Spirituality: *The Way is Within: A Spiritual Journey by Rathbun, R.*
Profit after commissions = $14.16.
My purchase cost = $1.50.

Gross profit margin = 844%.

CD's, DVD's, Video Games

My biggest profits from selling CD's, DVD's, and video games have come from selling more obscure titles that still have a decent amount of demand. You have to think, "what makes an item have a high resale value?". It is either because the item is new and in high demand or there is a limited supply of the item but still a large enough demand to keep the sales price afloat.

CD's

Legendary [Box Set] Ernest Tubb & Friends
Profit after commissions = $21.35.
My purchase cost = $1.75.
Gross profit margin = 1,120%.

Cat Stevens - Greatest Hits
Profit after commissions = $7.34.
My purchase cost = $0.50.
Gross profit margin = 1,368%.

Quidam by Cirque du Soleil
Profit after commissions = $14.55.
My purchase cost = $1.75.
Gross profit margin = 731%.

Night of Your Return by Fernando Ortega
Profit after commissions = $13.27.

My purchase cost = $1.00.
Gross profit margin = 1,227%.

Anthology by Joe Cocker
Profit after commissions = $13.06.
My purchase cost = $1.00.
Gross profit margin = 1,206%.

Nicolae: An Experience in Sound and Drama by Lahaye, T.
Profit after commissions = $12.65.
My purchase cost = $2.00.
Gross profit margin = 532%.

Walela by Walela
Profit after commissions = $11.10.
My purchase cost = $1.00.
Gross profit margin = 1,010%.

Music for Zen Meditation by Scott, T.
Profit after commissions = $10.97.
My purchase cost = $1.75.
Gross profit margin = 526%.

Cloud Dancers by Philip Elcano
Profit after commissions = $10.33.
My purchase cost = $1.75.
Gross profit margin = 490%.

From the Gekko by Daboa

Profit after commissions = $9.49.
My purchase cost = $1.00.
Gross profit margin = 849%.

DVD's

Close Encounters of the Third Kind (Two disc collector's edition)
Profit after commissions = $18.15.
My purchase cost = $1.75.
Gross profit margin = 9,371%.

Band of Brothers
Profit after commissions = $26.83.
My purchase cost = $3.50.
Gross profit margin = $667%.

Trainspotting
Profit after commissions = $15.01.
My purchase cost = $2.50.
Gross profit margin = 500%.

Stalingrad
Profit after commissions = $15.01.
My purchase cost = $1.75.
Gross profit margin = 757%.

Apocalypse Now
Profit after commissions = $13.71.
My purchase cost = $2.00.
Gross profit margin = 585%.

Taxi Driver (Collector's Edition)
Profit after commissions = $13.31.
My purchase cost = $2.50.
Gross profit margin = 432%.

Les Miserables
Profit after commissions = $12.04.
My purchase cost = $2.50.
Gross profit margin = 381%.

The Final Countdown
Profit after commissions = $10.86.
My purchase cost = $2.50.
Gross profit margin = 334%.

One Flew over the Cukoo's Nest
Profit after commissions = $10.33.
My purchase cost = $1.50.
Gross profit margin = 588%.

Best in Show
Profit after commissions = $9.45.
My purchase cost = $1.50.
Gross profit margin = 530%.

Video Games

Legend of Mana (Playstation)
Total profit after commission = $102.94.
My purchase cost = $1.00.

Gross profit margin = 10,194%.

I found this item brand new at a police auction. It was for an older video game console so it was out of print but still had a high demand. This has been my largest profit margin sale to date.

Dark Cloud 2 (Playstation 2)
Profit after commissions = $39.69.
My purchase cost = $1.50.
Gross profit margin = 2,546%.

Sid Meier's Civil War Collection (PC)
Profit after commissions = $18.24.
My purchase cost = $1.50.
Gross profit margin = 1,116%.

Warcraft III Battle Chest (PC)
Profit after commissions = $21.76.
My purchase cost = $5.00.
Gross profit margin = 335%.

Final Fantasy Tactics (Playstation)
Profit after commissions = $80.89.
My purchase cost = $1.50.
Gross profit margin = 5,292%.

Final Fantasy VII (Playstation)
Profit after commissions = $57.77.
My purchase cost = $1.50.

Gross profit margin = 3,751%.

The Neverhood (PC)
Profit after commissions = $38.85.
My purchase cost = $2.00.
Gross profit margin = 1,842%.

Sea Dogs (PC)
Profit after commissions = $23.88.
My purchase cost = $5.00
Gross profit margin = 377%.

APPENDIX 5:
GENERIC LISTING
TEMPLATES

If you are going to be using any of the automation techniques discussed in Chapter 7, then it is essential that you have a generic listing created for each grading condition that your item falls into. This way, when you upload your inventory into the automation program, you will select your condition grades, and then can copy your descriptions over based on that condition grade.

Even if you do not use an automation program to list products, it is helpful to have a generic listing description created for each condition grade. Doing so will enable you to simply copy and paste into each listing instead of having to re-create a specialized description for each product. I like to keep my listing descriptions short and to the point, but feel free to change or add to any template listed here.

Books

New: *Brand New Book! Ships same day or next business day.*
Like New: *Book is in excellent condition with no defects. Ships same day or next business day.*
Like New (Remainder Books): *Book contains remainder mark on outside edge. Pages are clean and spine is in excellent condition. Ships same day or next business day.*

Very Good: *Book is in very good condition with minimal wear. Ships same day or next business day.*

Good: *Book may contain limited notes and highlighting. Some wear to spine and/or cover. Ships same day or next business day.*

Good (Ex-Library): *Ex-library copy. Book may contain limited notes and highlighting. Some wear to spine and/or cover. Ships same day or next business day.*

Acceptable: *Considerable* wear to spine and cover. *Book may contain notes and highlighting. Ships same day or next business day.*

CD's

New: *Brand New CD in original seal. Ships same day or next business day.*

Like New: *CD is in excellent condition with no defects. Ships in original case with inserts. Ships same day or next business day.*

Like New (Remainder CD's): *CD contains remainder cut out on outside edge of jewel case. CD is in original seal. Ships same day or next business day.*

Very Good: *Jewel case may contain small cracks. CD is in excellent condition with no defects. Ships in original case with inserts. Ships same day or next business day.*

Good: *Some damage to jewel case. CD may contain small scratches but is playable. Ships in original case with inserts. Ships same day or next business day.*

Acceptable: *CD may contain scratches but is playable. Does not include original case or inserts. Ships same day or next business day.*

DVD's

New: *Brand New DVD in original seal. Ships same day or next business day.*

Like New: *DVD is in excellent condition with no defects. Ships in original case with inserts. Ships same day or next business day.*

Very Good: *DVD case shows minimal wear. DVD is in excellent condition with no defects. Ships in original case with inserts. Ships same day or next business day.*

Good: *Some damage to DVD case. DVD may contain small scratches but is playable. Ships in original case with inserts. Ships same day or next business day.*

Acceptable: *DVD may contain scratches but is playable. Does not include original case or inserts. Ships same day or next business day.*

Video Games

New: *Brand New game in original seal. Ships same day or next business day.*

Like New: *Game disc is in excellent condition with no defects. Ships in original case/box with inserts. Ships same day or next business day.*

Very Good: *Game case shows minimal wear. Game disc is in excellent condition with no defects. Ships in original case/box with inserts. Ships same day or next business day.*

Good: *Some damage to original case/box. Game disc may contain small scratches but is playable. Ships in original case/box with inserts. Ships same day or next business day.*

Acceptable: *Game Disc may contain scratches but is playable. Does not include original case/box or inserts. Ships same day or next business day.*

APPENDIX 6:
PROFIT ANALYSIS

Creating profit tables for each of the channels you will be selling on is crucial to understanding your break-even points and potential profit. Once you have your profit tables, you will have a better idea of how much you can afford to pay for items you are going to sell online.

I focused on an item sales price of $1.00 through $5.00 to give you an idea of how your profit will look at the low range of sales. As postage and commission rates can change, it is advisable to double check the current fee structure of all sales channels.

The profit tables are created using book sales as an example. The tables include all fees and commissions on the various sales channels except monthly fees. The tables also include a shipping supply cost of $0.35, a delivery confirmation fee of $0.19, and the current USPS Media Mail postage rate as of May 2009. The tables assume a shipping credit of $3.99 for Abebooks and eBay and also include all PayPal fees with items sold on eBay. Items in parentheses indicate a negative profit.

One interesting thing to point out is the profit of an Amazon.com Pro account compared to the profit when you sell a paperback book on Half.com; currently, the profit when selling a paperback on Half.com is the same as the profit when selling with an Amazon.com Pro account. The only difference is that you do not have to pay a monthly subscription to sell on Half.com but an Amazon.com Pro account will cost you $39.99

a month. The reason that it comes out the same even though the two sites charge different commission rates is due to the difference in shipping credit given between the two companies.

1 Pound Media Mail Rate

Sales Price	$1.00	$2.00	$3.00	$4.00	$5.00
Amazon (Standard)	($0.42)	$0.43	$1.28	$2.13	$2.98
Amazon (Pro)	$0.57	$1.42	$2.27	$3.12	$3.97
Half.com (Paperback)	$0.57	$1.42	$2.27	$3.12	$3.97
Half.com (Hardcover)	$1.00	$1.85	$2.70	$3.55	$4.40
Alibris (Basic)	$0.57	$1.57	$2.57	$3.47	$4.32
Alibris (Gold)	$1.57	$2.57	$3.57	$4.47	$5.32
Abebooks	$1.30	$2.24	$3.13	$3.99	$4.86
eBay (Fixed)	$0.73	$1.55	$2.37	$3.19	$4.01
eBay (Auction)	$1.09	$1.97	$2.86	$3.74	$4.62

2 Pound Media Mail Rate

Sales Price	$1.00	$2.00	$3.00	$4.00	$5.00
Amazon (Standard)	($0.81)	$0.04	$0.89	$1.74	$2.59
Amazon (Pro)	$0.18	$1.03	$1.88	$2.73	$3.58
Half.com (Paperback)	$0.18	$1.03	$1.88	$2.73	$3.58
Half.com (Hardcover)	$0.61	$1.46	$2.31	$3.16	$4.01
Alibris (Basic)	$0.18	$1.18	$2.18	$3.08	$3.93
Alibris (Gold)	$1.18	$2.18	$3.18	$4.08	$4.93
Abebooks	$0.91	$1.85	$2.74	$3.60	$4.47
eBay (Fixed)	$0.34	$1.16	$1.98	$2.80	$3.62
eBay (Auction)	$0.70	$1.58	$2.47	$3.35	$4.23

3 Pound Media Mail Rate

Sales Price	$1.00	$2.00	$3.00	$4.00	$5.00
Amazon (Standard)	($1.20)	($0.35)	$0.50	$1.35	$2.20
Amazon (Pro)	($0.21)	$0.64	$1.49	$2.34	$3.19
Half.com (Paperback)	($0.21)	$0.64	$1.49	$2.34	$3.19
Half.com (Hardcover)	$0.22	$1.07	$1.92	$2.77	$3.62
Alibris (Basic)	($0.21)	$0.79	$1.79	$2.69	$3.54
Alibris (Gold)	$0.79	$1.79	$2.79	$3.69	$4.54
Abebooks	$0.52	$1.46	$2.35	$3.21	$4.08
eBay (Fixed)	($0.05)	$0.77	$1.59	$2.41	$3.23
eBay (Auction)	$0.31	$1.19	$2.08	$2.96	$3.84

4 Pound Media Mail Rate

Sales Price	$1.00	$2.00	$3.00	$4.00	$5.00
Amazon (Standard)	($1.59)	($0.74)	$0.11	$0.96	$1.81
Amazon (Pro)	($0.60)	$0.25	$1.10	$1.95	$2.80
Half.com (Paperback)	($0.60)	$0.25	$1.10	$1.95	$2.80
Half.com (Hardcover)	($0.17)	$0.68	$1.53	$2.38	$3.23
Alibris (Basic)	($0.60)	$0.40	$1.40	$2.30	$3.15
Alibris (Gold)	$0.40	$1.40	$2.40	$3.30	$4.15
Abebooks	$0.13	$1.07	$1.96	$2.82	$3.69
eBay (Fixed)	($0.44)	$0.38	$1.20	$2.02	$2.84
eBay (Auction)	($0.08)	$0.80	$1.69	$2.57	$3.45

5 Pound Media Mail Rate

Sales Price	$1.00	$2.00	$3.00	$4.00	$5.00
Amazon (Standard)	($1.98)	($1.13)	($0.28)	$0.57	$1.42
Amazon (Pro)	($0.99)	($0.14)	$0.71	$1.56	$2.41
Half.com (Paperback)	($0.99)	($0.14)	$0.71	$1.56	$2.41
Half.com (Hardcover)	($0.56)	$0.29	$1.14	$1.99	$2.84
Alibris (Basic)	($0.99)	$0.01	$1.01	$1.91	$2.76
Alibris (Gold)	$0.01	$1.01	$2.01	$2.91	$3.76
Abebooks	($0.26)	$0.68	$1.57	$2.43	$3.30
eBay (Fixed)	($0.83)	($0.01)	$0.81	$1.63	$2.45
eBay (Auction)	($0.47)	$0.41	$1.30	$2.18	$3.06

APPENDIX 7: AMAZON BEST PRACTICES

Amazon.com does a great job of listing tons of helpful articles and tips on how to use their site. The following is from Amazon.com's article, "Best Practices". I would follow the policies listed when selling on Amazon.com and on any other website as well.

Best Practices
Listing Items and Inventory Management

- Update your online inventory daily to avoid stock-outs that may occur when an Amazon buyer purchases an item from you, but you no longer have that item on hand. Making updates is especially important if the inventory you are selling on Amazon Marketplace is also for sale through other venues.
- Before pricing your items, research prices for comparable products on Amazon Marketplace and make adjustments if necessary.
- If an item has been listed for more than 30 days and has not sold, check your pricing to make sure that it is competitive and make changes if necessary.
- The Vacation Settings feature may take up to 36 hours to remove your listings and another 36 hours to restore them. During this period, listings cannot be modified or deleted. Because of this, we do not suggest using this

feature to remove your listings from the site. Read more about using this feature by visiting the "Seller Account and Preferences" help page.

- For more information about listing on our site, please visit our collection of Help pages for "Listing Your Item".
- For information about inventory management, visit our page for "Managing and Relisting Your Items" or our related FAQ.

Additional Information for Pro Merchant Subscribers

- Break large Inventory Loader files into batches with fewer than 25,000 listings or file sizes smaller than 10 MB.
- It is not necessary to re-submit the same Inventory Loader file more than once; during peak times our systems can be very busy but be assured that we have received the file and it will be processed.
- After your file finishes processing, be sure to review the error log to determine why some of your listings may not have loaded.
- For more information about how to use Inventory Loader, please visit our page on "Volume Listing Tools".

Order Management

- Check your Manage Your Orders section regularly for important updates on your sales, rather than relying exclusively on e-mail notifications. You can access order information through your Seller Account.
- Provide high-quality customer service, which includes handling refunds and returns in a timely manner. Refund an order within 48 hours that you are unable to fill

and issue refunds for returns within five business days of receipt. You will find instructions on our "Refund Orders" page.

- Use the A-to-Z Guarantee only as a **last resort** when resolving matters with buyers. Multiple guarantee claims are an indication of seller performance problems.

Fulfillment

- Always ship your items within two business days of order notification. This is a requirement!
- Include a packing slip with your item. You can print it from your Seller Account or create your own. Do not forget to include your return address. Please also review our shipping and packing guidelines carefully.
- To understand shipping rates, visit our "Shipping Resources" page.
- Include a note with your package with your contact information and encourage your buyer to leave you feedback at **www.amazon.com/feedback**.
- Send buyers a ship confirmation e-mail after you have shipped their order, and include tracking or delivery confirmation numbers if they are available.
- For additional help with this topic, visit our Help pages for "Fulfillment, Getting Paid, and Feedback".

Customer Service

- Answer all buyer inquiries within 24 hours of receipt. Good communication with buyers promotes good feedback for sellers.
- Amazon.com was founded on providing an extraordinary experience for buyers. Customers have come to

expect this type of service, and that is what keeps them coming back for more purchases. We encourage you to use the reputation we've established to leverage your own business. As a seller, you are now in control of the same experience for your buyers: never lose sight of this philosophy.

Security

- Change your password regularly.
- Consider setting up a separate bank account for disbursements from your Marketplace Payments account.
- Amazon.com never asks you to verify sensitive information via e-mail. Submit such information only when completing an order on our website, registering for Marketplace Payments by Amazon, or contacting us directly through our online forms.
- Review the terms of our online "Privacy Notice" and our other "Privacy & Security" resources.
- If you are ever in doubt about the authenticity of an e-mail, visit our site directly by typing the address into your browser bar, rather than clicking any links. To find out more about Amazon.com's efforts to combat fraudulent e-mail, please visit our "Stop Spoofing" page.

Source: *www.Amazon.com*

APPENDIX 8:
RECOMMENDED
READING

Accounting for Non-Accountants: The Fast and Easy Way to Learn the Basics by Wayne Label (**Paperback** - Jun 1, 2006)

eBay 101: Selling on eBay For Part-time or Full-time Income, Beginner to PowerSeller in 90 Days by Steve Weber (**Paperback** - Jan 16, 2008)

eBay For Dummies (For Dummies (Computer/Tech)) by Marsha Collier (**Paperback** - Jul 7, 2009)

The eBay Seller's Tax and Legal Answer Book: Everything You Need to Know to Keep the Government Off Your Back and Out of Your Wallet by Cliff Ennico (**Paperback** - May 9, 2007)

How to Buy, Sell, and Profit on eBay: Kick-Start Your Home-Based Business in Just Thirty Days by Adam Ginsberg (**Paperback** - May 3, 2005)

How to Incorporate: A Handbook for Entrepreneurs and Professionals by Michael R. Diamond (**Paperback** - Jun 29, 2007)

Incorporate & Grow Rich! by Cheri S. Hill, Diane Kennedy, and C. W. Allen (**Paperback** - May 1, 2000)

Small Business For Dummies (For Dummies (Business & Personal Finance)) by Eric Tyson and Jim Schell (**Paperback** - Mar 4, 2008)

Small Business Start-Up Kit by Peri Pakroo (**Paperback** - Jan 30, 2008)

Small Time Business Operator, 10th Edition: How to Start Your Own Business, Keep Your Books, Pay Your Taxes & Stay Out of Trouble (Small Time Operator) by Bernard B. Kamoroff (**Paperback** - Jan 25, 2008)

Starting an Online Business For Dummies (For Dummies (Computer/Tech)) by Greg Holden (**Paperback** - April 16, 2007)

Tax Loopholes for eBay Sellers by Diane Kennedy and Janelle Elms (**Paperback** - Nov 1, 2005)

Taxes for Online Sellers by Simon Elisha (**Paperback** - May 28, 2007)

REFERENCES

1. Paypal.com. "About Us". Retrieved from:
   https://www.paypal-media.com/aboutus.cfm.
2. MSN.com. "Amazon.com Financial Results". Retrieved
   from:
   http://moneycentral.msn.com/investor/invsub/resul
   ts/statemnt.aspx?Symbol=AMZN&lstStatement=10
   YearSummary&stmtView=Ann.
3. Amazon.com. "Fees and Pricing". Retrieved from:
   http://www.amazon.com/gp/help/customer/display
   .html on.
4. Amazon.com. "Shipping". Retrieved from:
   http://www.amazon.com/gp/help/customer/display.
   html.
5. Amazon.com. "Condition Guidelines". Retrieved from:
   http://www.amazon.com/gp/help/customer/display
   .html.
6. Half.com. "Getting Paid". Retrieved from:
   http://pages.half.ebay.com/help/seller/get-paid.html.
7. Half.com. "Filling an Order". Retrieved from:
   http://pages.half.ebay.com/help/seller/get-paid.html.
8. Alibris.com. "Shipping Information". Retrieved from:
   http://www.alibris.com/help/shipping.
9. Alibris.com. "Alibris Fees: How Much Does It Cost to Sell on
   Alibris?". Retrieved from:
   http://www.alibris.com/sellers/program-fees.

10. Abebooks.com. "Subscription Rates". Retrieved from: http://www.abebooks.com/servlet/SubscriptionRatesP L.

11. eBay.com. "About eBay". Retrieved from: http://news.ebay.com/about.cfm.

12. eBay.com. "eBay.com Fees". Retrieved from: http://pages.ebay.com/help/sell/fees.html.

13. PayPal.com. "Transaction Fees for Domestic Payments - United States". Retrieved from: https://www.paypal.com/us/cgi-bin/webscr?cmd=_display-receiving-fees.

14. eBay.com. "eBay Stores Fees". Retrieved from: http://pages.ebay.com/help/sell/storefees.html.

15. USPS.com. "Prices". Retrieved from: http://www.usps.com/prices.

16. USPS.com. "Media Mail". Retrieved from: http://www.usps.com/send/waystosendmail/sendit withintheus/mediamail.htm.

17. Endicia. "Endicia Service Plan Pricing". Retrieved from: http://www.endicia.com/Pricing.

18. Stamps.com. "Help for Online Postage Software". Retrieved from: http://www.stamps.com/postage-online/faqs.

19. Investopedia.com. "Accrual Accounting". Retrieved from: http://www.investopedia.com/terms/a/acrrualaccounti ng.asp.

20. IRS. "Publication 334". Retrieved from: http://www.irs.gov/publications/p334/ch02.html#en_U S_publink100025118.

INDEX

A

A1 Overstock · 133
A1Books · 131
Abebooks.com · 40, 66–67, 131
Accounting · 128
Accrual Accounting · 128
Alibris · 63–65, 131
Alibris Basic · 63
Alibris Gold · 64
All-Scale · 138
AM Shipping Supplies Company, Inc. · 136
AMan Pro · 117
Amazon.com · 43–60, 131, 135, 137
Amazon.com Marketplace · 10
American Book Company · 133
Asellertool · 38, 138
Associated Bag Company · 94, 136
Atlanta Mail Recovery Center · 14
Audio Books · 29
Automation · 115

B

Baker & Taylor · 134
Bargain Books Wholesale · 133
Barnes & Noble · 131
Best Practices · 157
Bibles · 32
Biblio.com · 131
Blackthorne Basic · 121

Blackthorne Pro · 121
Book Sales · 15
Book Sales, Inc. · 134
Bookkeeping · 130
BookRouter · 118
Books · 23–32, 57, 139, 149
BookSaleFinder.com · 15
Books-a-Million · 131
Borders · 131
Boxes Cheaper · 136
Break-even Points · 153
Brick and Mortar · 9
Bubble Mailers · 92
Bulk Sales · 40
Business · 123
Buy.com · 131

C

Cash 4 Books · 40, 131
Cash Accounting · 128
Cash For CD's · 42, 131
Casual Seller · 2
CD's · 33, 57, 143, 150
Certified Public Accountant · 123
ChannelAdvisor · 119
ChannelMax · 118
CheapBooks · 131
Choosebooks.com · 132
Chrislands.com · 131
Classifieds · 19
Click-N-Ship · 90, 135
Collectible Books · 31
Collectible Coins · 13

Compass Packaging · 136
Complaints · 101
Corporation · 126
Corrugated Boxes · 92
Craigslist · 20, 132, 133
Customer Service · 99-108, 159

D

Daedalus Books Wholesale · 134
DBA · 126
DEAauctions.com · 14
Dictionaries · 32
Domestic Shipping Rates · 84
Donation Centers · 11
DVD Pawn · 41, 132
DVD's · 34, 57, 145, 151

E

Easy-fold Mailers · 92
eBay · 16–19, 42, 68–81, 132, 133,
    136, 137
eBay Store · 74
ecampus.com · 41, 132
Electronics · 36
Encyclopedias · 32
Endicia · 87, 135
Estate Sales · 8
esupplystore.com · 137
EZ Shipping Supply · 136

F

Fast-Pack.com · 137

Feature Fees · 74
FedEx · 86
Feedback · 79, 106
Feedback Score · 99
Fiction · 30
FillZ · 117
Final Value Fees · 70
First-Class Mail · 86
Fixed Price Listing · 71
Fulfillment · 159
Full-time Business Seller · 3
Furniture · 36

G

Garage Sales · 6
Gemm · 132
Generic Listing · 58
Generic Listing Templates · 149
Goodwill · 10
Grading Conditions For Books · 53
Grading Conditions For CD's · 54
Grading Conditions For DVD's · 55
Grading Conditions For Video Games
    · 56

H

Haggle · 7
Half.com · 60–62, 78, 132
HomeBase · 66, 120

I

Ingram Book Company · 134

Ingram Entertainment, Inc. · 134
Insertion Fees · 69
Internal Revenue Service · 128
Inventory · 109
Inventory Label · 111
Inventory Management · 157
ISBN · 41
Item Description · 100

J

JustShippingSupplies.com · 136

L

Labels · 94
Library Auctions · 16
Library Sales · 15
Limited Liability Company · 125
Listing · 48, 157
Listing Software · 15
Love For Books · 134

M

Mail Extractor · 119
Mass Market Hardcovers · 26
Mass Market Paperbacks · 24
Media Mail · 85
Mediascouter · 38, 138
Monster Packaging · 137
Mountain View Movies · 134

N

Negative Feedback · 107
New Items · 21
Newspapers · 16
Non-Fiction · 31
Northern Safety & Industrial · 137

O

Office Depot · 136
OfficeMax · 137
Online Postage Companies · 87
Order Management · 158
OurShippingSupplies.com · 137
Overstock · 132

P

PackagingPrice.com · 136
PackagingSupplies.com · 136
Packit Right · 137
Padded Mailers · 92
Paper Mart · 136
Partnership · 125
Part-time Business Seller · 3
PayPal · 17, 62, 66, 68, 91, 135
PennySaver · 6
Pitney Bowes · 90, 135
Police Auctions · 11
Post Office Auctions · 14
Postage · 83
Pre-Order Reports · 37
Price Adjusting · 113
Priority Mail · 86
Pro Merchant Account · 44

Pro Merchant Seller Account Fees · 47

Problem Deliveries · 105

Profit Margin · 21

Profit Tables · 153

PropertyRoom.com · 13, 133

Public Storage · 113

Q

QuickBooks · 130

Quicken · 130

Quill · 136

R

Refunds · 105

Remainder Books · 21

Remainder CD's · 22

Remainder Mark · 22

RepriceIt · 119

Resale Certificate · 127

Return Policy · 101

Returns · 101

Rigid Mailers · 92

S

Sales Tax Permit · 127

Salvation Army · 10

San Diego · 12

SaveOnScales.com · 137

Scale · 89, 95

Scales Galore · 138

ScalesOnline.com · 137

Scanners · 15, 37, 121

Scoutpal · 38, 138

SecondSpin.com · 42, 132

Security · 160

Sell My DVD's · 41, 132

Sell.com Classifieds · 132

Seller Community · 59, 65, 67, 80

Seller Engine · 119

Seller Magic · 120

Selling Manager · 120

Selling Manager Pro · 120

Shipment Confirmation · 100

Shipping Credit · 46

Shipping Supplies · 91

ShippingSupply.com · 94, 136

SKU System · 109

Society of CPA's · 123

Sole Proprietorship · 125

Stale Inventory · 111

Stamps.com · 89, 135

Standard Auction · 69

Standard Seller Account · 43

Standard Seller Account Fees · 45

Staples · 136

State Tax Board · 21

Stealth Postage · 84, 87

Storage · 112

Storage Rental Auctions · 20

T

Tax · 130

Textbooks · 28

TextbooksRus · 132

Textbookx · 132

The Book Depot · 134

The Box Company, Inc. · 137

Thermal Printer · 88, 95
Thrift Stores · 10
Trade Hardcovers · 28
Trade Paperbacks · 27
Turbo Lister · 120

U

U.S. Government Property · 14
U.S. Treasury Auctions · 14
U.S. Treasury Department · 133
Uline · 94, 136
Undeliverable · 14
UPS · 86
Used Bookstores · 9

V

Valore Books · 132
Video Games · 34, 57, 146, 151

W

Wholesale & Bulk Lots · 18

Y

Yard Sales · 6

About the Author

Patrick Leo is an author and professional online seller. Formerly an auditor for a Certified Public Accounting firm, he began selling used items online in 2003. He found selling online to be so profitable that he started a home-based business and has been able to sell from the comfort of his home ever since. He specializes in selling used books, CD's, DVD's, and video games and has sold items on every major sales channel on the Internet; including Amazon.com, eBay.com, Half.com, Alibris.com, and Abebooks.com.

Patrick Leo holds a Bachelor of Science degree in the field of Business Finance from the University of Phoenix. He currently resides in Southern California. You can send him an e-mail by referencing his name or this book's title and sending it to: p_lpublications@yahoo.com. In addition, you can visit www.pandlpublications.com for further information.

Breinigsville, PA USA
18 February 2010
232780BV00001B/23/P